**The Cook Book**

©2018 Meze Publishing Ltd. All rights reserved.

First edition printed in 2018 in the UK.

ISBN: 978-1-910863-46-6

Thank you to: Michel Roux Jr.

Compiled by: Kate Bourne, Harriet Kerly,
Caroline Kings (www.carolinekings.com), Severien
Vits
and Charlotte Rogers

Written by: Katie Fisher

Photography by: Severien Vits
(www.severienvits.myportfolio.com)

Designed by: Matt Crowder, Paul Cocker

Contributors: Jessica Findlow

Cover art: Dan Smith
(www.bionicgraphics.co.uk)

Printed by: Bell & Bain Ltd, Glasgow

tree of
HOPE

The fundraising charity supporting
children's healthcare needs

me:ze
PUBLISHING

Published by Meze Publishing Limited

Unit 1b, 2 Kelham Square

Kelham Riverside

Sheffield S3 8SD

Web: www.mezepublishing.co.uk

Telephone: 0114 275 7709

Email: info@mezepublishing.co.uk

# FOREWORD

As a boy born in Kent, I champion this book and the wonderful stories it tells. As a chef, I cannot express enough how important local producers are and how each one should be celebrated. The tales of our local producers, restaurants, café owners, pubs, delicatessens, restaurants and farm shops are what build and nurture communities and make each one so beautifully unique and magical.

I might be biased, but I believe that it is food that brings people together in a way that so few other things can. Through food we can create together, eat together, talk together and put the world to rights! Each recipe and story in this book lovingly threads together a community and all in order to raise money for a vital cause.

The need for charities such as Tree of Hope is becoming ever more important. The work that Tree of Hope does is so crucial for children and families across the nation and it is hugely important that we all continue to support them.

Let's get cooking, and let's keep supporting the people of West Kent!

*Michel Roux Jr.*

Preparation time: 30 minutes, plus 12 hours freezing | Serves: 10

# Michel Roux Jr.

# ICED RED BERRY SOUFFLÉ

This dish always impresses and is well worth the effort. It can be made as little individual soufflés or one big one to share. If the berries are very sweet and ripe, you can cut down the sugar in the recipe by ten percent.

## Ingredients

1kg mixed berries
(e.g. strawberries, raspberries, blueberries, blackcurrants)
400g caster sugar
1 lemon, juiced
4 egg whites
500ml water
80ml whipping cream
**To serve:**
500g mixed berries, plus extra to decorate
100g caster sugar

## Method

Hull and, if necessary, wash the fruit. Blend with 150g of the sugar, then pass through a fine sieve. Add lemon juice to heighten the taste if required. Prepare ten individual soufflé dishes (9cm diameter and 6cm deep) by tying a piece of greaseproof paper around the outside edge of the dish to form a collar that stands 5cm above the rim.

Put the egg whites into the bowl of an electric mixer. In a perfectly clean saucepan, dissolve the remaining 250g of sugar in the water over low heat. When the sugar has completely dissolved, bring to the boil, skim off the foam and heat until the syrup reaches 120°c on a sugar thermometer. Beat the egg whites until foamy, then, with the whisk still running, pour the hot syrup directly on the egg whites, avoiding the beaters. Continue beating until the meringue is cool.

Whip the cream until soft peaks form and fold into the fruit pulp. Delicately fold in the meringue, then spoon into the prepared soufflé dishes. Freeze for 12 hours.

### To serve

Decorate with fresh berries and, if you like, serve with a sauce made by puréeing 500g berries with the caster sugar, sharpening the taste with a little lemon juice if needed.

# Tree of Hope

Tree of Hope has been empowering families for over 25 years to obtain the specialist treatment, therapy and equipment their seriously ill or disabled child so desperately needs. We aim to transform the life of every child we support by providing them with the medical care that would otherwise be unavailable to them.

Tree of Hope supports over 800 children nationwide every year. For every child we support, we know there are 1000 more that may need our help. The Cook Book – Sevenoaks, Tonbridge & Tunbridge Wells will help Tree of Hope not only raise vital funds, but also raise awareness so that we can reach more families and transform their lives too.

---

### Louis

Louis has quadriplegic cerebral palsy which means he requires lots of specialist therapy and equipment that allows him to stay healthy and increase his independence. His family came to Tree of Hope in 2014 and has been supported ever since by the charity, ensuring they can obtain what Louis needs to thrive.

"With the help of Tree of Hope we have been able to fundraise for intensive physiotherapy, hydrotherapy, equipment and adaptions to our home, all things that are not always readily available. Tree of Hope takes the pressure off us as a family; they manage all our funds, and are always on the end of the phone when we need them! We are so grateful to them. Without the support from Tree of Hope and our amazing friends and family, Louis wouldn't be where he is now."

*Jody, Louis' mum*

### Kallie

Eight-year-old Kallie has congenital heart disease and cerebral palsy. Tree of Hope supported her to raise £40,000 for a life changing operation that would enable her to walk independently. Under a year after her operation Kallie took her very first unaided steps.

"Without the support of the Tree of Hope team Kallie would not be where she is today."

*Charlie, Kallie's mum*

### Richie

Richie wanted the ability to reach his full potential and move freely around his home and garden. His family came to Tree of Hope to raise £10,000 for a power chair that would allow him the independence he deserves.

"To everyone at Tree of Hope, thank you so much for advising us, supporting us and most of all for helping us to make Richie's dream come true! His new power chair is fabulous."

*Jo, Richie's mum*

tree of **HOPE**

*The fundraising charity supporting children's healthcare needs*

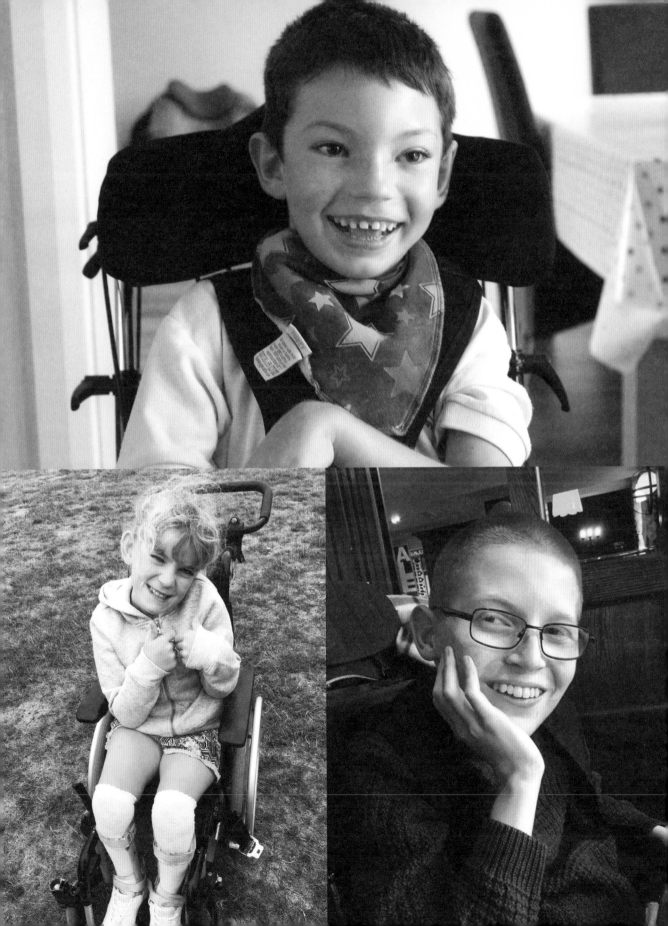

# DINE AND DONATE

Dine and Donate is Tree of Hope's annual campaign, bringing people together to hold foodie events at home or at work and raise vital funds for Tree of Hope.

---

From dog walking brunches, to prosecco afternoon teas, curry nights, FA Cup Final parties, wine tasting dinners and movie nights to anything else you can think of, the more inventive the better!

In its first year, the campaign saw hundreds of supporters host and attend events throughout the spring and early summer, raising over £11,000 for Tree of Hope and enabling us to transform the lives of more seriously ill and disabled children in the UK.

Hosting your own Dine and Donate event is easy. Simply sign up at www.dineanddonate.uk to receive your Host Pack and hold your own event between March 1st and May 31st.

Find out more at www.dineanddonate.uk

# THINKING OF HOSTING YOUR OWN FOODIE EVENT?

See the recipes below for inspiration!

---

**Seafood Celebration**

*Little Brown Jug* – Roasted fillet of cod with Jerusalem artichokes, mussels and chorizo (page 141)

*Vittle and Swig* – Spiced cod cheeks with labneh and salt baked beetroot (page 129)

*Rustled Up* – Dressed crab, tomato salad, consommé, squid ink cracker (page 99)

**Afternoon Tea**

*Cocolicious* – Salted caramel lamingtons (page 35)

*Wholefood Wakeup* – Marbled berry cashew cake (page 145)

*Bore Place* – Courgette and tomato chutney (page 31)

**Brunch**

*Severien Vits* – Granola with puffed quinoa and chocolate chips (page 115)

*Daily Bread* – Harissa spiced avocado and poached egg (page 39)

*Sulston's* – Kentish strawberries, watermelon, chia and coconut smoothie (page 125)

**The Perfect Dinner Party**

*The King's Head* – Sautéed asparagus spears, poached free range egg, glazed hollandaise, shaved wiltshire truffle (page 137)

*The Small Holding* – Roast duck with gooseberry and courgette (page 119)

*Michel Roux Jr.* – Iced berry soufflé (page 7)

**Curry Evening**

*Fuggles Beer Café* – Chickpea curry with turmeric flatbreads and yoghurt dressing (page 51)

*Sankey's* – A banging simple curry (page 107)

**The First Summer BBQ**

*Sankey's* – BBQ oysters (page 109)

*Basil* – Roast potato, green bean and semi-dried tomato salad (page 23)

*Jane Beedle* – No churn ice cream (page 67)

**Cocktail Party**

*Framptons* – Signature bloody mary (page 47)

*The Poet at Matfield* – M & H lemon elderflower cocktail (page 87)

# THE FRUITS OF OUR LABOUR

It's a common sight, as you drive through West Kent, to see roadside stalls, with handwritten signs selling local fruit and veg. Asparagus, cherries, strawberries and cobnuts are typical wares for sale but if you venture away from the main highways and head for the byways, you'll find an abundance of farm shops with overflowing shelves.

Kent is one of the warmest parts of the UK and it's thanks to its hot summers and fertile landscape that crops grow so well and have done for hundreds of years. Indeed, it's believed that it was King Henry VIII who gave the county its famous moniker of the 'Garden of England' after being treated to a delicious bowl of Kent cherries. These days, 90% of English cherries are grown in Kent; they are one of our most popular exports, alongside plums, strawberries, apples and pears.

Plentiful fruit has inspired 'cottage industries' through the ages. These days, in West Kent, the likes of Charrington's of Matfield, cider and apple juice producers and Turner's Cider of Marden are capitalising on the bounty of their own gardens, with other juice and alcoholic drinks producers spanning the county.

And in Kent we don't just produce the fruit and veg box staples, such is the diversity of our countryside. Kent spirits' producer, Greensand Ridge, can find the eight botanicals that are added to the distillery's distinctly flavoured signature-gin within a mile of the site: cobnuts, gorse, oak moss, honey, rosehips, hawthorn berries, bay laurel and poppy seeds. Sustainability is also critical to this producer, using local growers' damaged, not-good-enough-for-the-supermarket raspberries and apples to make its Raspberry Ghost eau de vie and apple brandy.

The clement Kent weather is ideal for grape cultivation and the south east is now home to many vineyards with award-winning Mount Vineyard and Squerryes being just two based in West Kent, both specialising in sparkling wines. And how could I not mention this area's rich brewing history? The Kent horizon has its own frothy top made up of white oast house cowls, taking us back to a time when hop-picking attracted London workers to the area in autumn for a 'working holiday'.

Today West Kent is home to numerous breweries including Westerham Brewery and Tonbridge Brewery and we have our very own beer cafés! Fuggles may sound like a peculiar word but it's actually the name of a type of hops used for brewing and the name of West Kent's beer cafés, one in Tonbridge and one in Tunbridge Wells. Check out their chapter on page 46.

Nowadays, many Kent farmers' crops are bought by the major supermarkets and transported around the UK and beyond so that others can enjoy the fruits of Kent's labour. But with the provenance of our food becoming increasingly important to us all, alongside a willingness to reduce our carbon footprints and a desire to return to a bygone era of seasonal eating habits, people like to buy local. Local chefs, and those involved in the food and drink industry have a similar mindset; Will Devlin of The Small Holding in Kilndown grows many of his own ingredients in his restaurant garden (check out his recipe on page 119).

Whether you're a man or maid of Kent, a Kentish man or maid, eating in or dining out, you'll be spoilt for choice by the quality of the produce on offer in our county.

*Caroline Kings - Food Blogger, Eat Around Tonbridge*

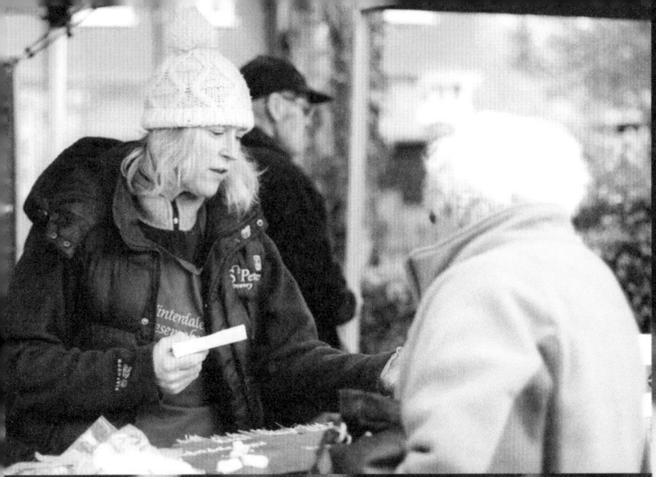
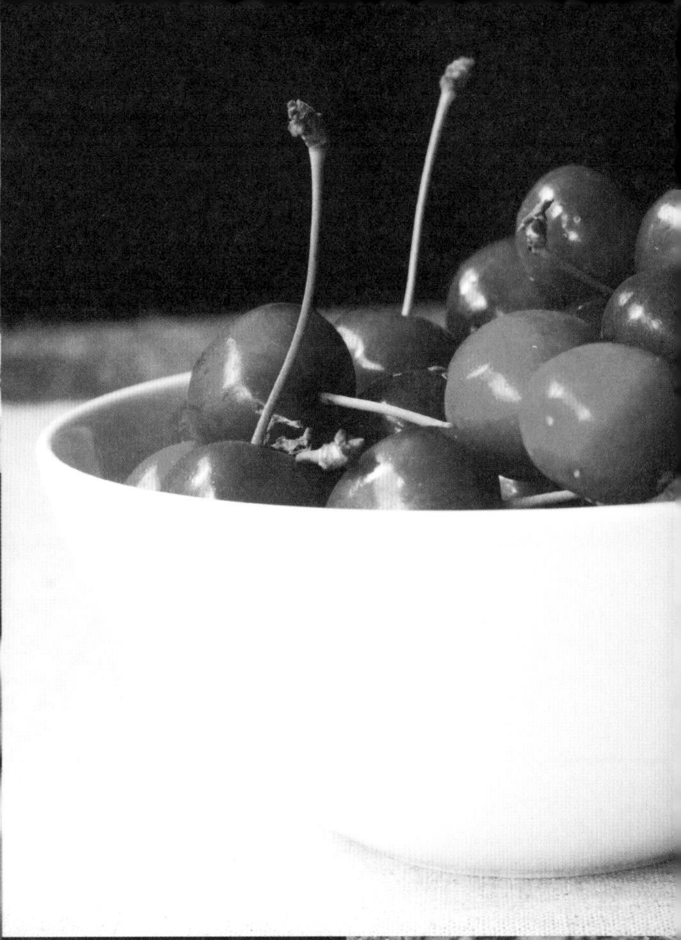
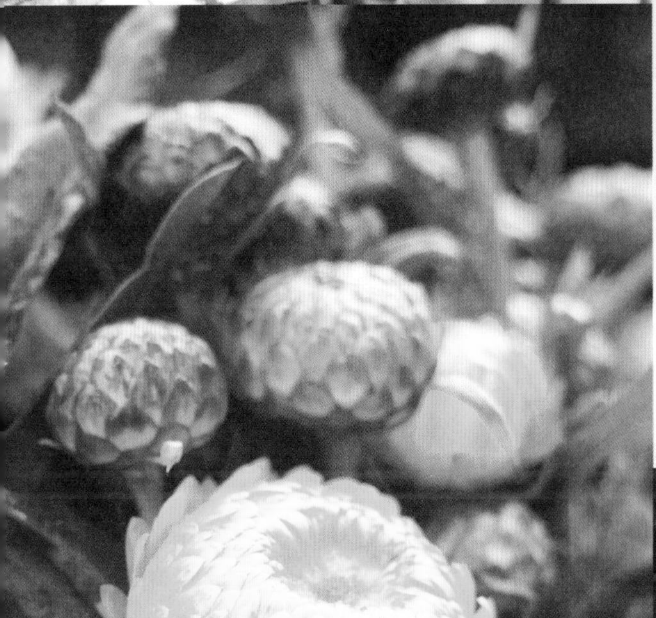
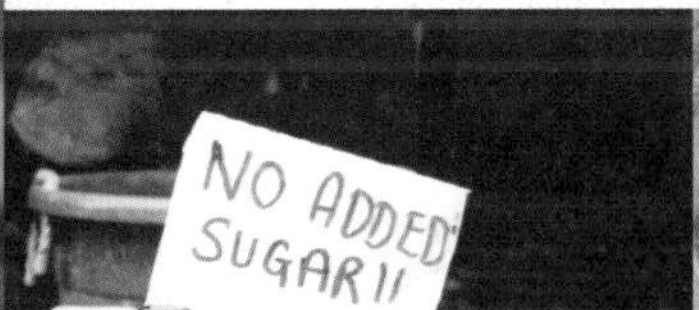
NO ADDED
SUGAR!!
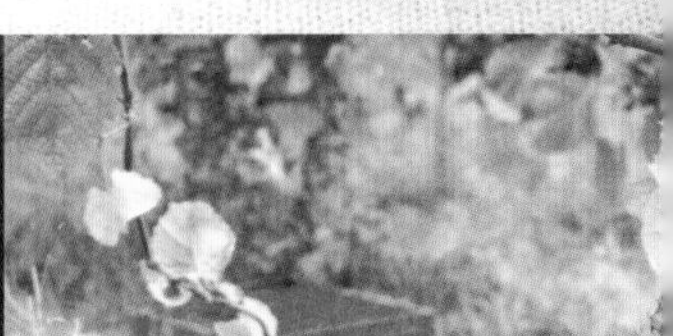
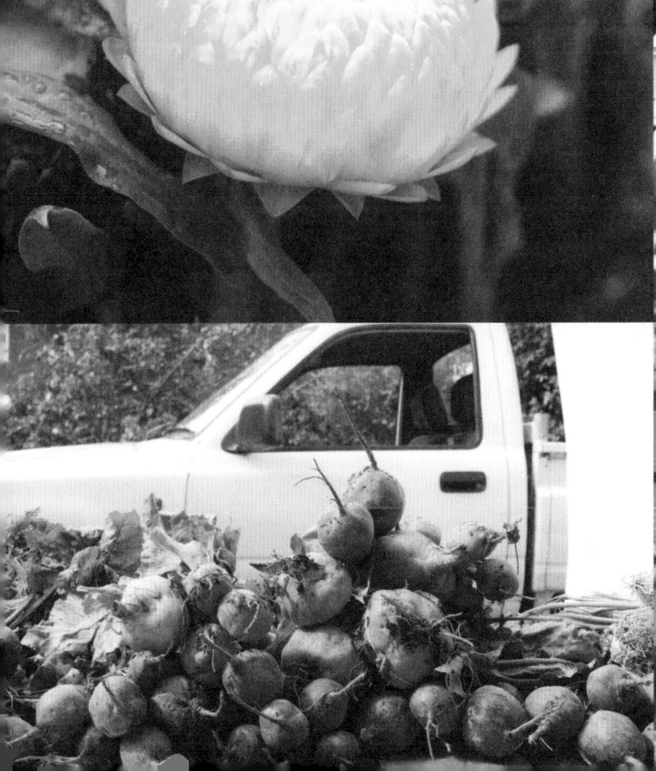
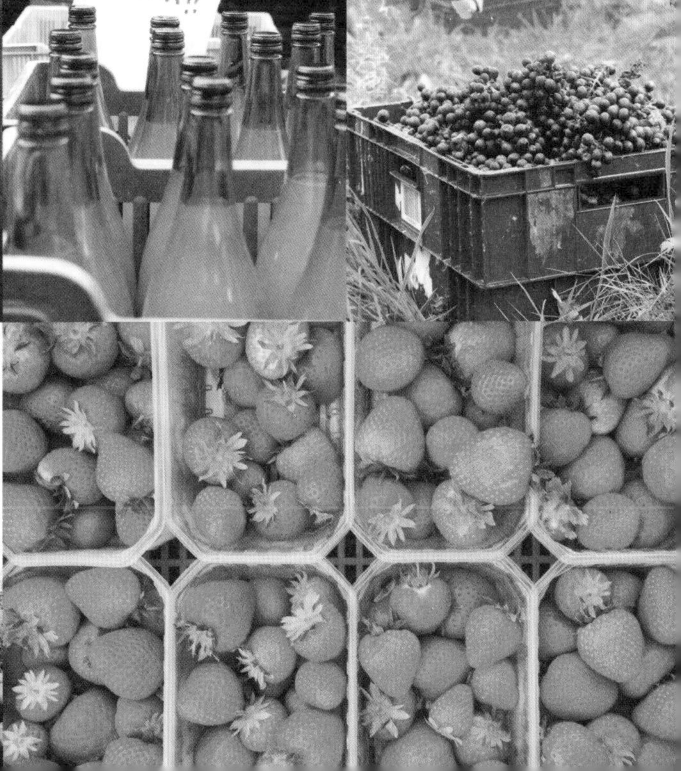

# The Contents

# WHOLE HEARTED GOODNESS

Full of flavour, vibrant colours, and the best local produce; Basil's food and drink is second to none when it comes to fresh and exciting wholesome food and indulgent cakes.

---

Siblings Matthew Castle and Julia Ehren are the driving force behind Basil, a venture that grew out of their philosophy and love of wholesome food and indulgent cakes. The business launched in 2008 with the first café in Tunbridge Wells, and was met with such enthusiasm from locals that a second Basil took up residence in the town centre. Behind the scenes, 'Basil to You' began to flourish as well, delivering freshly prepared food to other businesses, private parties and special events with signature flavour and quality.

Three more cafés have since joined the Basil family, but despite all the exciting expansions, ensuring consistency in the quality of the food and drink remains paramount for Matthew and Julia. Everything is freshly made in the Tunbridge Wells central production kitchen — Julia's domain, shared by her daughter Juliana, who has taken the cakes to "a whole new level" says Matthew — and delivered to all five cafés each morning, so that customers can be greeted by a display of beautiful sweet treats, a counter full of fresh salads and quiches and a mountain of handmade sausage rolls.

"People do eat with their eyes," says Matthew, "so it's important to Julia that when she creates the food it looks just as good as it tastes." The lunches and afternoon treats are complemented by speciality coffee, roasted in Kent, and juice made from the garden of England's fruit trees. Basil uses as many local suppliers as possible, supporting the area through promoting and celebrating its incredible produce. Fullers Farm Shop is the team's go-to for free-range meat, local grocer Oliver Greens delivers fresh fruit and vegetables each day and all the eggs used in the food are free-range from the Five Chimneys Farm in Hadlow Down.

The attention to detail and commitment to quality at Basil hasn't gone unnoticed; another two Great Taste awards joined the ranks in 2018 for the café's gluten-free hazelnut and pomegranate cake and the vegan mixed fruit tartlet. It was designated Best Kent Café by Muddy Stilettos in the same year, and has a Tunbridge Wells 'Coffee Shop World Cup' for the mantelpiece. "We've been on such a great journey so far, but we're still looking forwards," Matthew says. "No matter where we go next though, Basil will always be about family, friends, and fantastic food!"

Roasted Butternut Squash, Chilli and toasted Seeds Filo tart

Preparation time: 15 minutes | Cooking time: 45-50 minutes | Serves: 10 (generous portions)

# ℬASIL

# GREEN BEAN, ROASTED POTATO AND SUN-DRIED TOMATO SALAD

This is one of our favourite vegan and gluten-free salads, mostly because it is so versatile. Perfect as a cold salad in summer, or just as good as a hot veggie addition to any meal. We love using loads of fresh herbs in our cooking. Fresh oregano can be a little tricky to get hold of in some supermarkets, if you can't find any, just add a couple of pinches of dried oregano instead. We hope you love this recipe as much as we do; it's easy to make and tasty so what's not to love!

## INGREDIENTS

1kg good quality Maris Piper or red potatoes

6 cloves of garlic

1 bunch of fresh oregano

1 bunch of fresh basil

Olive oil

Salt and pepper

120g sun-dried tomatoes (keep the oil for the dressing)

750g green beans

**For the dressing:**

1 lemon

50ml olive oil

1 tbsp sugar (use any kind you like; we like coconut sugar)

**To serve:**

1 bunch of chives

## METHOD

Preheat the oven to 200°c. Peel and slice the potatoes in half lengthways, in half again lengthways and then cut horizontally to get roughly 2cm cubes. Finely chop all the garlic and set half aside for the dressing. Take the leaves off the oregano stalks and finely chop along with half the basil. The stalks of the basil are fine to use as they are soft. Add the garlic and the chopped herbs to the potatoes along with a generous drizzle of olive oil and some salt and pepper. Mix together, making sure the potatoes are evenly covered and glistening. Transfer the potatoes into a roasting tin and roast in the preheated oven for roughly 30 to 40 minutes or until golden brown and crispy. Roughly chop the sun-dried tomatoes, remembering to keep the oil for the dressing. Place the green beans in boiling water for around 3 to 4 minutes. Refresh under cold water to retain the greenness.

### For the dressing

While the potatoes are roasting, combine the chopped garlic you set aside earlier, the zest and juice of the lemon, olive oil, sugar and a little bit of the sun-dried tomato oil in a jug. Whisk together and adjust the flavour to taste.

### To serve

Roughly chop the chives along with the remaining basil. Place the roasted potatoes and green beans in a bowl and toss together along with the herbs, dressing, sun-dried tomatoes and a pinch more salt and pepper. Present on a sharing platter and let everyone dive in!

# KEEP THE FIRE BURNING

The Beacon is a restaurant in the heart of the Kent countryside, its private dining rooms,
bar and outdoor terrace boasting stunning views.

Tucked away by the edge of the woods, The Beacon is a former Arts & Craft country house, built in 1895, with panoramic views across Happy Valley and 17 acres of seemingly endless gardens, full of foxgloves, wild herbs and wildlife. When Pete and Viv Cornwell first bought The Beacon in 2014, the site was a little run down and neglected but they worked hard to transform the house back to its former glory, full of character and rustic charm, while protecting all the original features. There are cosy corners and candlelight, snugs and roaring fires in the winter and in the summer, guests can relax under the pergola vines or in the shade of the pomegranate tree on the terrace.

If you take a walk after lunch you'll see vegetable beds growing salads, beets, carrots and herbs for the kitchen garden, the chicken run where fresh eggs are gathered daily, and The Beacon's own beehives from which unique honey is produced. Executive chef Mark Constable's style of well-sourced and simply prepared food with twists of flavour and spicing is a natural complement to the garden kitchen setting at The Beacon. When not in the kitchen,

Mark can be found in the vegetable patch, foraging for wild ingredients in the woods and Happy Valley or poring over vegetable seed brochures for the soon-to-arrive poly tunnels. "The food is all about simplicity but focused on flavour," he says, "and what we aim for is just great food."

The Beacon is part of the hospitality group I'll Be Mother, led by Pete Cornwell, which includes The Twenty Six and The Swan at Chapel Down. He has been in the hospitality industry for over 30 years, from his initial training in the Swiss Alps to running the day-to-day operations and vision of I'll be Mother, and has a passion for quality and excellence. "The customer experience and seeing people enjoying dining with us is something I'm really passionate about, but it is the people I work with and the whole I'll Be Mother family who make me most proud," he says. I'll Be Mother is about celebrating things that get better with time, and from the seasonal menus to the stylish yet rustic interiors of The Beacon, Kent has plenty to look forward to yet.

Preparation time: 30 minutes | Cooking time: approx. 4 hours | Serves: 4

# THE BEACON

# SLOW COOKED LAMB WITH HARISSA ROAST AUBERGINE

Lamb breast is a great partner to the warmth of North African spicing, and is one of the least expensive and most flavourful cuts. This dish needs nothing except perhaps some garlic yoghurt and a few flatbreads to mop up the delicious sauce.

## INGREDIENTS

**For the lamb:**
1.6-1.8kg lamb breast
Sea salt and black pepper
4 tbsp ras el hanout
Bunch of mint, chopped
A little olive oil
8 green cardamom pods, lightly crushed
5 bay leaves
2 cloves of garlic, crushed
1 litre stock, preferably lamb
6 tbsp honey, preferably local Kent honey

**For the aubergines:**
2 medium aubergines, diced
3-4 tbsp olive oil
50g harissa (Belazu is a good brand)
2 cloves of garlic
Bunch of flat leaf parsley, chopped
4 baby aubergines

**For the apricot sauce:**
4 fresh apricots
30g sugar
1 sprig of thyme

**For the bulgur wheat:**
250g bulgur wheat
1 litre vegetable stock

**To finish:**
Fresh pomegranate seeds
Chopped mint and coriander

## METHOD

### For the lamb

Ask your butcher to bone the lamb breast and ask to keep the bones.

Heat the oven to 150°c. Flatten the lamb breast, season with sea salt and freshly ground black pepper and rub in the ras el hanout and freshly chopped mint. Roll up and tie with string into a long roll; it should resemble a Swiss roll. Lightly smear olive oil all over the lamb and seal on a very hot griddle (or barbecue) to get a smoky flavour. Char the lamb rib bones alongside the breast. Once golden brown, transfer everything into a casserole dish and add the cardamom pods, bay leaves, garlic. Cover with lamb stock and the lid and cook low and slow in the oven. After 3 hours of cooking, push a skewer into the lamb. It should meet little resistance and be tender. Leave for another hour if the meat needs longer.

Once the lamb breast is cooked, remove from the casserole, cover with foil and keep warm. Pick the meat from the lamb ribs and keep for later. Remove the rib bones from the stock, add the local honey and reduce until the sauce is a good consistency.

### For the aubergines

Gently roast the diced aubergines in a frying pan with a little of the harissa paste, olive oil and chopped garlic. Cook until soft and slightly charred on the edges and finish with chopped flat leaf parsley. For the baby aubergines, criss-cross the bottom of each aubergine, rub with olive oil and a small amount of harissa. Cook in the oven with the lamb, until soft and tender but holding their shape.

### For the apricot sauce

Cut each apricot into wedges then sprinkle with the sugar and add the thyme sprig. Roast for 20 minutes in a hot oven until soft. Remove the thyme and blend until smooth with a little white wine or a splash of water.

### For the bulgur wheat

Simply cook in boiling vegetable stock, following the instructions on the packet.

### To finish

Slice the warm lamb breast into portions. Gently combine the bulgur wheat, picked rib meat and the lamb sauce.

If serving family style, use a large dish or platter to serve the diced aubergine, baby aubergine and slices of lamb with the bulgur wheat and sauce over and around everything. Spoon the apricot purée onto the plate and finish with the pomegranate seeds, chopped mint and coriander.

# BACK TO NATURE

Bore Place provides people from all walks of life with the opportunity to connect with nature at a beautiful historic venue set amidst 500 acres of Kentish countryside.

---

The connections between nature, food, learning and sustainability are brought to life at Bore Place, home to the Commonwork Trust, a charitable organisation, and a centre for environmental and outdoor learning. The 500 acre estate encompasses an organic dairy farm and market garden, as well as unspoilt countryside that's open for people to enjoy all year round. The trust, directed by Caroline Arnold, has many branches that spread from its core ethos, which focuses on bringing people back to nature and contributing to positive change by modelling sustainable ways of working and living. From schools to artisanal producers, Bore Place enables others to become part of that change through events, programmes, farm and woodland walks, and even stays in the Grade II listed Bore Place House where guests can sample the organic fruit, vegetables and cheese produced on the estate and prepared by the resident chef.

This wonderful range of produce includes the award-winning Edmund Tew, created by Blackwoods Cheese Company with milk from Bore Place's organic dairy farm and crowned Supreme Champion at the 2018 Artisan Cheese Awards. Dave Holton and Tim Jarvis are the cheesemakers behind its success, and their company is one of several complementary businesses working on site at Bore Place. Metske van der Laan grows organic fruit and vegetables for the venue, organic box schemes and wholesalers, The Organic Cakery produces bespoke wedding cakes using organic produce, Free Range Glamping offers short stays on the farm, and the woodland itself, which also fuels the dairy and buildings via a woodchip-fed biomass boiler, is lovingly cared for by John Waller, a woodsman and traditional craftsman who runs courses in the Green Wood Workshop.

The programme of public events at Bore Place, detailed in the What's On section of the website, is a great way to try something new, from astronomy to vegan cookery and bat walks to basketry. Bore Place Walks have made the countryside both on and surrounding the estate accessible, celebrating Kent's countryside and wildlife. Opportunities are available to anyone wanting to contribute to Bore Place, whether that's a company looking to give back to their local community or a student wanting a work placement on the farm.

The trust's founding principles were established by Neil and Jenifer Wates, who bought the estate in 1976 to connect people with the land and its wonderful produce, sharing and promoting the benefits of living and working sustainably for a greener and happier future, and these values remain as important today as they were over 40 years ago.

Courgette & tomato
chutney

www.boreplace.org

...es, courgettes, onions, apples, sultanas, caraway
...llow mustard seeds, cloves, juniper berries, cider
...inegar, cinnamon, demerara sugar, water

Preparation time: 25 minutes | Cooking time: 1 hour 30 minutes | Makes: 18 200g jars

# BORE PLACE

# COURGETTE AND TOMATO CHUTNEY

The Bore Place organic market garden has an abundance of both courgettes and tomatoes. This is a really easy recipe and a delicious taste of summer to enjoy over the cooler months. It makes a terrific Christmas present to enjoy with cheese. At Bore Place, young people make this as a learning activity and it is always enjoyed by our guests.

## INGREDIENTS

1kg plum tomatoes
1kg courgettes
4 onions
4 apples
300g sultanas
2 tbsp caraway seeds
2 tbsp yellow mustard seeds
2 tbsp ground cloves
2 tbsp juniper berries
2 tbsp ground cinnamon
500ml cider vinegar
500g Demerara sugar
300ml water

## METHOD

Cut the fruit and vegetables into ½cm cubes, then place the spices, cider vinegar and sugar in a saucepan and bring to the boil. Add the diced fruit and vegetables and simmer for 1 hour and 30 minutes. Keep an eye on the chutney as it simmers and add the water as needed if it starts to catch.

Meanwhile, sterilise your jars and lids. We do this by putting them on a hot wash in a dishwasher and then drying them out gently in an oven preheated to 100°c. Fill the jars with the cooked chutney and screw the lids on tightly. The chutney should keep for up to 12 months. Once you have opened the chutney, keep in the fridge and eat within a week.

# IN THE PINK

Combining delicious yet nutritious brunches and lunches with sweet treats, Cocolicious is a cosy kitchen centred on a passion for coffee, food, and cake that's served with love.

Sweet by name and sweet by nature, Cocolicious is a celebration of delicious food and drink. The patisserie café menu balances nutritious salads and savoury plates with plenty of cake, hot chocolate, proper ice cream milkshakes and – crucially, of course – top-notch coffee. Owner and founder Loulou saw a gap in Cranbrook that needed filling with a friendly daytime café, so she set up the business with her husband Andrew in 2013 on the back of a successful catering venture operated from her home. The couple initially moved to Kent to give their young children space to grow up in, but fell in love themselves with the beautiful countryside that also happened to be a "fantastic area for local produce," as Loulou was delighted to discover.

A chef for many years, Loulou was keen to source these local ingredients to use in her cooking and baking. She loves to experiment so is constantly devising new delights by drawing on her previous travels for work, her training in Switzerland, and her home country, Kenya. Her signature lamingtons are an Australian treat that have been stocked by Selfridges, and there are new specials from the patisserie counter to be discovered daily. Loulou bakes and cooks alongside her two longest-serving members of staff, Ginny and Sarah, who replied to an ad she put in the local paper and have been with her since day one. "I couldn't have done it without them, and they've become part of the family here," says Loulou.

The trio also make bespoke cakes for special occasions and parties of all kinds. Quality is always paramount, so everything for the café and catering is freshly made – even the icings, jams, sauces and more – in the Cocolicious kitchen. From the bright décor, which reveals Loulou's fondness for pretty pinks and clean Scandinavian interiors, to the perfectly poured cups of coffee (the whole team have trained as baristas to make sure they get it just right) the experience has been created with careful attention to detail. "We really want our customers – many of whom we have developed lovely relationships with as they visit regularly – to feel at home here," says Loulou. Health and treating yourself never looked or tasted so good!

Preparation time: 60 minutes | Cooking time: 40 minutes | Makes: 16

# ℭOCOLICIOUS

# SALTED CARAMEL LAMINGTONS

This sweet treat has delighted Aussie taste buds for over 100 years and now even has its own national day! The classic lamington is filled with jam and dipped in a chocolate icing, but we'd like to share one of our best sellers with you. Salted caramel, sponge cake and coconut... you really can't go wrong!

## INGREDIENTS

**For the sponge:**
4 eggs
100g sugar
1 tsp vanilla essence
100g flour
¼ tsp baking powder
50g butter, melted

**For the salted caramel:**
200g caster sugar
100g unsalted butter
125ml double cream
1 tsp Maldon sea salt

**For the caramel dip:**
150ml single cream
150g salted caramel
150g white chocolate, roughly chopped into small pieces
500g desiccated coconut

## METHOD

**For the sponge**

Preheat the oven to 180°c. Grease and flour a 20cm by 20cm baking tin, lining the base with parchment paper. Beat the eggs, sugar and vanilla in a large bowl with a hand mixer or in a Kitchen Aid on a medium to high speed until pale and thick, around 5 to 8 minutes. Sift the flour and baking powder over the egg and sugar mixture and use a rubber spatula to gently combine. Add the melted butter in two parts, gently mixing with a rubber spatula until completely combined, then pour the mixture into the prepared tin.

Bake for 25 minutes, or until a skewer inserted into the middle of the cake comes out clean. Turn the cake out onto a wire rack and then, once cooled, cut into 5cm by 5cm squares. You can refrigerate the cake for a few hours or leave the cake overnight in an airtight container. Slightly less fresh cake will be easier to dip in the caramel.

**For the salted caramel**

Heat the sugar in a medium saucepan over a medium heat, stirring constantly with a wooden spoon. The sugar will form clumps and then eventually melt into a thick amber liquid as you continue to stir. Once the sugar has completely melted, immediately add the butter, taking care as the caramel will bubble rapidly. Stir until the butter has completely melted, about 2 to 3 minutes. Use a metal whisk if it's separating. Drizzle the cream into the caramel while stirring and then boil for about 2 to 3 minutes, while stirring, until smooth. Remove from heat and stir in the salt. Pour into a jam jar to store.

**For the caramel dip**

Place the chopped white chocolate into a heatproof bowl. In a saucepan, bring the cream and caramel to the boil. Once boiling, pour immediately over the white chocolate and stir continuously until all the chocolate has melted.

When you are ready to dip the cakes, set up an area large enough to accommodate the cake pieces, the caramel dip, the coconut and a baking tray lined with baking parchment on the work surface, in that order. Using a fork or your hands, dip the cake cubes into the caramel dip to completely coat them. Let any excess mixture drip off the cakes then place them into the coconut and roll them around lightly to coat evenly. Set the cake cubes on parchment paper once rolled.

**To serve**

You can refrigerate the cakes to help the icing set. Bring them to room temperature before serving. Delicious with freshly brewed coffee or tea and some extra salted caramel on the side!

# CRUST ME, I'M ON A ROLL!

Daily Bread is a café with a twist: fresh food produced on site and bread baked daily in the micro-bakery by one passionate man and his team, who love to create a welcoming atmosphere and food for the whole family to enjoy.

From a young age, Daily Bread's founder Joe McElroy was interested in food and drink, having spent many of his younger years working in his local village pub. With no formal training, Joe cooked for fun while at university, enjoying being creative with food and adding little twists to classic recipes for friends and family. After completing his studies Joe took his passion for all things culinary to the next level, working at a range of cafés and restaurants, as well as completing a summer season working for a travelling catering company. This diverse experience led him to open the doors to Daily Bread in 2013.

Joe takes a hands-on approach to the business, getting stuck in to everything. If you can't see him on the floor, you'll find him in the kitchen cooking up a storm or discussing new ideas with the team, while ensuring the quality of the food and the attention to detail that they pride themselves on is always delivered. What's unique about the café is that all of the food is made from locally sourced ingredients on site. "Doing things from scratch feels more genuine and interesting" says Joe.

After attending a bread making course at the School of Artisan Food on the Welbeck Estate, Joe decided to turn one of the café's outbuildings into a micro- bakery in 2017. Fresh homemade bread is now baked on a daily basis, to be used for the breakfasts and lunches in the café, and has become one of the attractive features that keep customers coming back. Other local establishments have now started buying the freshly made bread on a wholesale basis.

Since opening, Daily Bread has been nominated for a variety of awards, including Best Independent Café at the Kent Life Food and Drink Awards 2017, and it was also a Muddy Stillettos 2018 finalist. Joe aims to keep Daily Bread moving forward, creating new meals, recipes and menus for the public to enjoy, and he is also hoping to help the environment by adding solar panels to the bakery roof as its main source of power in the near future!

Preparation time: 10 minutes | Cooking time: 10 minutes | Serves: 2

# DAILY BREAD

# HARISSA SPICED POACHED EGGS & AVOCADO

This is one of our most popular breakfast dishes. It's fairly quick and easy to prepare and looks great on the plate!

## INGREDIENTS

1 tbsp harissa
Olive or rapeseed oil
4 sun-dried tomatoes
1 avocado
Large handful of rocket
100g feta
Distilled malt vinegar
4 eggs
Sourdough bread
Salted butter
Salt and pepper

## METHOD

In a mixing bowl, combine the harissa with a splash of oil. Chop the sun-dried tomatoes up with scissors and add to the bowl. Slice the avocado and add to the bowl with the rocket and feta. Gently fold together so everything is evenly dispersed.

Bring a large pan of water to boil and add a glug of the vinegar (this helps to keep the whites together when poaching the eggs). Once the water is boiling, pop the bread into the toaster or under the grill. Obviously our sourdough from Daily Bread is ideal! Just use your favourite bread though. Crack the eggs and gently slide them into the water, getting as close to the surface as possible.

Once the toast is done, spread with plenty of salted butter and evenly divide the avocado mixture between the slices on two plates.

Lift the eggs out of the water with a slotted spoon and pat dry with kitchen towel. Place the eggs on top of the avocado mix, season with salt and black pepper, then enjoy!

# SERVED WITH MILITARY PRECISION

British brasserie-style food, great cocktails and coffee, a warm welcome for the community, and a beautifully renovated Georgian building meet at Framptons in Tunbridge Wells' historic centre.

---

The founders of Framptons, Tom Walker and Sam Westlake, launched their journey into hospitality from a very different background. They met in the army and left with a shared hunger to try something new of their own. From the very beginning the aim was for Framptons to embrace quality local ingredients, convert interesting historical buildings, and create a sense of community in the casual dining space.

The Tunbridge Wells café bar and kitchen was the second Framptons venue, but first total refurbishment, located at the entrance to the Pantiles in a Grade II listed former bank that dates back to the 17th century. Tom and Sam kept the original features to maintain the integrity of the building, as well as allowing them to design a unique theatre kitchen upstairs and a bar on the ground floor that looks into the old vault. They also brought together a team of many talents, including the general manager and mixologist, James Harrison, who is classically trained and previously worked at some of the world's most highly acclaimed bars.

The kitchen team is led by head chef Rob Theron, whose training includes working at the world's 22nd best restaurant, as well as a restaurant with two AA rosettes in Kent. Rob's ethos fits in perfectly at Framptons: sourcing the best local, seasonal produce (from within a 20 mile radius where possible) and serving dishes in a simple yet classical style to really showcase the ingredients. Rob's skills as a pastry chef are also strongly reflected in the dessert menu. British brasserie-style dishes comprise the brunch, lunch and dinner offering; the concept behind Framptons' food is something all day for everyone, reflecting the founders' commitment to accessible, family friendly dining alongside the fantastic range of craft beer, real ale, wine, spirits and of course, cocktails.

Creating a place for the local community was at the forefront of Tom and Sam's ambitions with Framptons, which is one of the reasons they chose Tunbridge Wells. "People are really open to trying new things here, and have been so welcoming," says Tom. "We were awarded Best Independent Restaurant by the Times of Tunbridge Wells just one year after opening and we're proud of the whole team who provide great service, great food, and a place to be enjoyed by all."

Preparation time: 10 minutes | Cooking time: 8 minutes | Serves: 4

# FRAMPTONS

# WAKAME CRUSTED BAKED HAKE

A milder, more delicate member of the cod family, hake is in season for seven months of the year and goes perfectly with our choice of seaweed and sea herbs. This is a simple recipe by our head chef, Rob Theron, that brings the flavour of the fish to the fore and will offer something a little different at home. For us, it represents everything our kitchen is about: an interesting combination of quality seasonal produce.

## INGREDIENTS

160g unsalted butter
16g wakame seaweed, washed
4g garlic
5 hake fillets (150g-180g each)
12 clams
80ml dry white wine
1 tbsp finely chopped flat leaf parsley
80g samphire
8g sea purslane

## METHOD

Pulse the butter, seaweed and garlic together in a blender until smooth. Place the hake fillets on a baking tray and top each one with a tablespoon of the seaweed butter. Bake for 8 minutes in the oven at 180°c fan.

While the hake is in the oven, heat the clams in the white wine and parsley until the clams open fully. Add the sea purslane and samphire and take the pan off the heat.

Remove the cooked hake from the oven and allow to rest for 1 minute. Place the clams, herbs and sauce in a bowl and place the hake on top to serve.

Cooking time: 15 minutes | Serves: 8

# FRAMPTONS

## CLASSIC LEMON CURD

We think this is the most amazing lemon curd, and so we wanted to share it with you. When you know how to make this curd, you can use it in different ways and very easily impress your friends and family!

### INGREDIENTS

4 whole eggs
4 egg yolks
200g unsalted butter
125g caster sugar
4 lemons, zested and juiced
100ml double cream

### METHOD

Combine all the ingredients except for the cream in a heavy-bottomed pan. Place over a gentle flame and keep stirring until the mixture comes to a thick custard texture. Remove from the heat, whisk in the cream and allow to cool.

Brilliant served with berries or pavlova. You can also store this in a sterilised jar in the fridge for up to 2 weeks, that way you can dip in and enjoy whenever!

Preparation time: approx. 20 minutes | Cooking time: 3 hours | Serves: 1

# FRAMPTONS

# SIGNATURE BLOODY MARY

Everyone knows what a Bloody Mary is but let's be honest, it's rarely that good. That's why Framptons' general manager James Harrison decided to create something very special out of an absolute classic. Don't let this ingredients list put you off because once you've made a batch of the seasoning and spice mixes, the rest is easy and you'll be fully prepared to nurse any hangover or entertain your friends for brunch. This is the best Bloody Mary you'll ever have.

## INGREDIENTS

**For the vegetable juice:**

1 shallot

2 cloves of garlic

Dash of olive oil

1 carrot

2 sticks of celery

1 cucumber

Salt and pepper

Dash of red wine

Dash of veal stock

3 litres tomato juice

500ml beetroot juice

500ml carrot juice

**For the drink:**

50ml vodka

200ml vegetable juice

50ml seasoning mixture

1 level tsp spice mix

1 level tsp truffle and mushroom ketchup

1 level tsp coriander and basil pesto

1 level tsp green tomato chutney

Pickled, raw and charred vegetables

## METHOD

First, make your vegetable juice. Sweat the shallot and garlic on the hob in olive oil until translucent and then add the carrot, celery, cucumber and any other vegetables you may want to use up that day. Season with salt and pepper. Deglaze the pan with a little red wine until the wine has almost completely evaporated and repeat this process with veal stock. Add the tomato juice, beetroot juice and carrot juice. Bring to the boil and simmer for approximately 3 hours until the mixture takes on the consistency of a passata. Check the seasoning and strain into a bottle.

For the seasoning mix, we blend Worcester sauce, various sherries, sherry vinegar, cornichon vinegar, bitters, smoke and soy sauce. Play around with different combinations to find what works for you. Alternatively, use any vinegar-based hot sauce.

The spice mix we use at Framptons is a closely guarded secret. What we can say is that we use 80 different ingredients to achieve the desired flavour profile, heat and complexity we're after. For you guys at home the following will work very nicely: four parts smoked paprika, one part cayenne, one part sugar, one part smoked salt and one part black pepper.

We make ketchup, pesto and chutney ourselves in the kitchen at Framptons but you can buy quality examples of these to make life a little easier at home. If you do want to make these yourself, pop in and see us for the complete recipes.

**To make the drink**

Add all the ingredients into a steel shaker or large jug. Stir the mixture to dissolve the spices and seasoning until the contents are well integrated. Roll the mixture with ice to combine, chill and aerate while retaining texture. Single strain (not a fine strain) into a glass with ice.

Garnish with pickled and raw vegetables of your choosing. We also use a blow torch on vegetables like baby corn for great flavour and that impressive final flourish!

# A CURE FOR ALL ALEMENTS

Craft beer, British charcuterie, cheese and wine, coffee, and friendly cafés make for the perfect place to hang out and enjoy good food, drinks and company in Kent.

Fuggles Beer Café was created in 2013 with the aim of specialising in the best British and European beers founder Alex Greig could find. At the time, there was nothing else like it and good craft beer was hard to find, so Alex just wanted to provide somewhere relaxed and welcoming where the finer things in life could be appreciated. These soon included a carefully curated wine list, spirits, and food including local charcuterie, fine cheeses, and a few tasty options whipped up in the café despite the lack of a kitchen! The venture has grown fast since its first location took off in Tunbridge Wells, with a second opening in Tonbridge four years later and a growing team who remain passionate about their products.

Alex, Doug and Dan head up the business and make sure that the original ethos still runs through every aspect of what they do. Concentrating on small breweries and putting an ever-changing line-up of 22 beers and ciders in each café means that Fuggles can promote independent producers and introduce people to things outside the mainstream. This extends to the ingredients they source for their hand-picked and regularly changing menu, working on recommendations to find the best suppliers and supporting the great partnerships they have formed with companies like Crown & Queue Meats, Neal's Yard Dairy, MONS Cheesemongers and Cobble Lane Cured to name just a few.

Putting the effort into finding and promoting these hidden gems is totally worth it for Alex and the team, because they can ensure what they sell is of the best quality and also let their customers know exactly what they're eating and drinking. Having a hands-on knowledge of their products is very important at Fuggles. The aim isn't for the beer cafés to be merely a place to drink for the sake of drinking, but somewhere to enjoy the craft of great brewers and fellow food lovers amongst friends. Making them accessible and spearheading innovative approaches are key goals for the team; having pints available in thirds, introducing 'crowlers' – litres of beer canned on site to take away or enjoy at the festivals Fuggles attend – and welcoming anyone from age 18 to 80 keeps the business moving and the beer flowing.

CASK £4.10 SNAILS BANK 'APPLE + GINGER' (Herefordshire)
M PINT Smooth + sweet blend of ginger

TONBRIDGE COPPERNOB

EVENTS @ FUGGLES
· BEER · CAFE ·

MEET THE CRUMBER – CRUMBS BREWING
3rd
7pm

TONBRIDGE CALLING – AFTERPARTY!!
4th Aug
From 8pm

VINYL REVOLUTION POP UP RECORD STORE DAY
SUN
5th
AUG

Preparation time: 30 minutes | Cooking time: 30 minutes | Serves: 4

# FUGGLES

# CHICKPEA CURRY WITH TURMERIC FLATBREADS AND YOGHURT DRESSING

At Fuggles we don't have a fully equipped, working kitchen so we need to be inventive when conceiving dishes as well as finding exceptional produce to showcase. We cook this curry in a soup kettle so if making at home on a stove, use the lowest heat possible. The extra time lets the flavours blend together really nicely. We came up with this dish to honour a visit from our friends at Bundobust, an Indian street food and craft beer restaurant.

## INGREDIENTS

**For the flatbreads:**

300g strong white bread flour

1 tbsp turmeric

Pinch of Maldon sea salt

25g dried yeast

200ml warm water

1 tbsp extra-virgin olive oil

**For the curry:**

1 tbsp vegetable oil

8 dried Kashmiri chillies

1 tbsp coriander seeds

2 660g jars of Navarrico Garbanzos chickpeas

1 tbsp turmeric

1 tsp tamarind extract

100g creamed coconut

1 tbsp brown mustard seeds

2 tsp Kashmiri chilli powder

5 curry leaves

3 roasted red peppers, sliced

**For the yoghurt dressing:**

100g natural yoghurt

1 tbsp ground cumin

Pinch of Maldon sea salt

2 tbsp extra-virgin olive oil

**To serve:**

Fresh coriander

## METHOD

**For the flatbreads**

To make your dough, put the flour, turmeric and salt into a mixing bowl. Add the yeast to the warm water and whisk until fully dissolved. Pour the liquid into the bowl a little at a time while kneading the mixture constantly. You want a tacky dough; not wet, not dry. Add the olive oil and knead for another couple of minutes. Cover the bowl and leave to prove for at least 20 minutes.

**For the curry**

To roast the peppers yourself, char the skin all over by placing the pepper directly on the flame of the hob or under a hot grill, then wrap fully in cling film and leave for 5 minutes. Unwrap the peppers, peel off the charred skin and discard the seeds and core. Most roasted peppers in jars will be too bitter for this dish, but if you are using them we recommend piquillo peppers for their sweetness.

Heat the vegetable oil on a low heat for at least 2 minutes. Add the dried chillies and coriander seeds and fry until aromatic (the point where you can smell the heat of the chilli). Transfer the chillies and seeds to a pestle and mortar using a slotted spoon and pound them into a paste. Add the drained chickpeas and turmeric to the pan the chillies were in and mix well. Mix the tamarind extract with the chilli and coriander paste, then pound in the creamed coconut until it has the consistency of a shop-bought curry paste. Stir this paste into the chickpeas along with the mustard seeds, chilli powder, curry leaves and the sliced roasted peppers. Leave the mixture to cook away for 15 minutes.

Meanwhile, divide the flatbread dough into pieces the size of golf balls and roll each one out as thin as possible (our minimum thickness is around 2mm) and dry fry them in a hot pan. This only takes seconds if the pan is hot enough.

**For the yoghurt dressing**

Simply whisk together all the ingredients and thin with a little water if necessary.

**To serve**

Garnish the finished curry with a few fresh coriander leaves, serve the hot flatbreads on the side, and enjoy.

# A CUT ABOVE

Fuller's Butchers and Farm Shop is a family business, run with dedication to quality local produce and pride in the best customer service for over 45 years.

The butchers in Hawkenbury was where it all began for the Fullers. In 1972, the business opened its doors and has been serving the food lovers of Tunbridge Wells and the surrounding area ever since. The now late Tony Fuller ran the shop with his wife Margaret, who kept the business on from 1984 until their son Steve, who trained at Smithfield College, took over. Steve is the owner of Fuller's today and has built a reputation on his father's legacy for quality meats produced by local farmers at both the butchers and the farm shop just a mile out of town, which he opened with his wife June in 2014. With Steve and June's children alongside his sister Sarah helping out, it's the definition of a thriving family business!

The farm shop at Eridge sells all the products available at the butcher's shop, from a full range of locally sourced meats to freshly made pies and pasties, alongside a wonderful array of artisan products such as handcrafted cheeses and wines from Kent's own vineyards. Fruit and vegetables are delivered daily by a supplier based in the area, and deli items such as Scotch eggs and sausage rolls come directly from the butchers where they are prepared and baked in-house. The shop is a foodie's treasure trove, and even has a selection of gifts including biscuits and chocolates. "You could come in and pick up everything for a meal here, including dessert and drinks," says June.

Whatever their many regular customers pop in for, the team's emphasis at both the butchers and farm shop is always on finding the best quality produce available and providing a generous helping of excellent customer service along with it. Being part of the local community is really important to Steve, by going that extra mile to engage and support the area through its people. There are eight highly skilled butchers at Fuller's who can offer advice and cooking tips on any cut of meat, fully prepared from the carcass, which comes in whole, with expertise. A host of apprentices are continuing the trade for the next generation, and dedicated front of house staff are always ready with a warm welcome. "We consider ourselves very lucky to have them all," say June and Steve, "and couldn't do what we do without everyone."

Preparation time: 10 minutes | Cooking time: approx. 2 hours | Serves: 6

# FULLER'S

# ROAST RIB OF BEEF WITH YORKSHIRE PUDDINGS

If you asked any of our friends and family what our favourite roast dinner would be, the answer would always be roast beef. The cut we would choose is a well-hung Sussex rib of beef; not only does it look good but it tastes fantastic too.

## INGREDIENTS

2½ kg rib of beef

Olive oil

Salt and pepper

**For the Yorkshire puddings:**

170g plain flour

170ml milk

115ml water

2 large eggs

Salt and pepper

## METHOD

Preheat the oven to 220°c fan. Massage the whole joint with olive oil and season lightly all over with salt and pepper. Place in a large roasting tin and pop into the oven for 25 minutes or until the meat is well browned and sizzling. Turn the oven down to 150°c and continue to cook for 15 to 20 minutes for every half a kilogram depending on how well done you like your beef. We always use an ovenproof temperature probe and cook our beef to a core temperature of 50°c for a medium rare joint. Once the beef is cooked, remove it from the oven, cover loosely with foil and leave the meat to rest for at least half an hour.

While the meat is resting, we like to use a gravy separator for the meat juices. The fat can be used for delicious Yorkshire puddings, while the succulent juices enhance the flavour of the gravy. To make extra-large Yorkshires, we like to use a muffin tin.

### For the Yorkshire puddings

Pop all the ingredients into a large mixing bowl and whisk vigorously to ensure that the batter is lump free. Turn the oven up to 220°c. Add a little of the fat from your gravy separator into the muffin tin, heat in the oven and when the fat is bubbling, pour the pudding batter equally into the muffin tin. Cook them on the top shelf of your oven for 20 to 25 minutes.

### To serve

When carving the meat, I run the knife down the back of the ribs to release the meat from the bone. Turn the meat on its side, carve into thin slices and then arrange on your plate with the Yorkshire puddings and a good helping of roast potatoes, seasonal vegetables, and gravy. Enjoy!

# THE SIMPLE THINGS IN LIFE

In the midst of picturesque countryside lies the beautiful hamlet of Charcott, and here you will find a little gem of a pub serving unbeatably local food and drink: The Greyhound Charcott.

---

Owned and run by Fran and Rich since March 2017, The Greyhound Charcott is about great local food and drink enjoyed with family and friends in a cosy, friendly, welcoming pub. The couple are local to the area and had their eye on the venue for a while, so when they finally got the opportunity to buy the freehold it was a no brainer, but also a leap of faith. Fran had worked for another fantastic local pub before, but opening their own place was a new adventure for them both.

Rich is passionate about food, though, and had the perfect set up to create a seasonally led menu using his family farm just two miles from the pub, where he rears and butchers livestock. The kitchen uses Dexter beef, pork and lamb alongside locally available produce — including regular gluts of vegetables from a friendly neighbour — in dishes that are made from scratch by Rich and his two chefs. He and Fran devise the menus between them, which cover light lunches and inventive veggie food to Sunday roasts and, of course, plenty of Kentish beer and cider.

As a place to sit and enjoy a drink, The Greyhound Charcott stands out for its commitment to the best. As Fran says, "I'm not keen on big brand names or products that can be found in every other pub; we avoid those in favour of making the effort to find unusual and unique independents." Larkins is the nearest brewery at just two miles from the pump, but the drinks offering is always evolving so guests can discover new favourites. This ethos applies to the wine list — featuring varieties from Kent's own vineyards — and the selection of gins. Even the bar snacks come from within the county; the Kent Crisps are particularly popular.

The couple know many of their customers now, as people from Charcott and its surrounding villages have made The Greyhound their local and built up good relationships with the team. Giving their pub a relaxed, traditional feel has been so important to Fran and Rich. The unique ambience is often remarked on, something which they're both very proud of, and the TripAdvisor Certificate of Excellence received on their one year anniversary of opening was a great bonus!

Preparation time: 1 hour 30 minutes | Cooking time: 15 minutes | Serves: 6

# THE GREYHOUND CHARCOTT

## STIDOLPHS SPICY LAMB BURGER WITH FETA AND TZATZIKI

One of Rich's favourites and a great tasting burger, made with fresh lamb from his own flock on his own farmland, just two miles from our pub. The careful blending of spices flavours the delicious meat before shaping it by hand into burgers, which are topped with tasty homemade tzatziki and tangy feta cheese.

### INGREDIENTS

**For the burgers:**
1kg fresh lamb mince
1 medium red onion, finely diced
2 cloves of garlic, peeled and minced
1 tsp chilli powder
1 tsp ground cumin
1½ tsp oregano
1 tsp flaked sea salt
1 tsp ground black pepper
1 tbsp fine breadcrumbs
1 tbsp olive oil

**For the tzatziki:**
1 small clove of garlic
1 tbsp good quality olive oil
½ a large cucumber
500g plain Greek yoghurt
1 tsp fresh mint, finely chopped
1 tsp fresh dill, finely chopped
1 tbsp freshly squeezed lemon juice
½ tsp flaked sea salt

**To serve:**
6 brioche burger buns
6 slices of feta cheese
6 baby gem lettuce leaves
6 slices of beef tomato

### METHOD

**For the burgers**

Combine the lamb mince with the red onion, garlic, spices, salt, pepper, breadcrumbs and olive oil. Use both hands to ensure that everything is evenly distributed. Dip or rinse your hands in cold water and then divide the mince mixture into six equal portions of 180g each. Having wet hands makes shaping the mince into compact balls much easier. Flatten each ball out into a burger patty with your palms ensuring each once is the same thickness, about 2cm is perfect. Place into a plastic box, separated with greaseproof paper if stacking, and place the box into the fridge to set for a least 1 hour prior to cooking.

**For the tzatziki**

Crush and finely chop the garlic then mix with the olive oil in a bowl large enough for all the ingredients. Leave to infuse. Slice the cucumber lengthways down the middle, then use a teaspoon to gently scrape all the soft seeds out, leaving just the pale flesh and skin. Grate the cucumber onto a tea towel, and then wrap the cucumber up to wring out the excess water. Add the cucumber to the mixing bowl with the garlic oil and add the yoghurt, mint, dill, lemon juice and sea salt. Mix thoroughly and place in the fridge until ready for serving.

When ready to cook, take the burgers out of the fridge. Heat a teaspoon of olive oil in a griddle or frying pan on a medium heat, then wait until the pan is hot before carefully placing the burgers in. Press gently down on each burger with a spatula to get a good colour as they cook, turn over after 5 to 6 minutes and repeat on the other side. The total cooking time should be no more than 12 minutes. Remove from the heat and rest the burgers for 2 minutes.

**To serve**

Slice the buns in half and lightly toast under the grill. Top each base with one tablespoon of the fresh tzatziki, top with a burger and then add the slice of feta, a baby gem lettuce leaf and a slice of beef tomato. Finish with the toasted bun tops and you're ready to serve. Our favourite accompaniments to these burgers are a portion of sweet potato fries and fresh dressed salad. Serve up and enjoy!

# A WORLD OF FLAVOUR

Flavours from international cuisines come together at the skilled hands of the two award-winning chefs who established Gurkha Planet.

Gurkha Planet serves food from around the world, with a particular emphasis on traditional Indian and Nepalese dishes, made by two acclaimed and highly experienced chefs. Dinesh Maharjan and Daya Ram Giri worked together for more than a decade when they decided to set up their own business and opened the relaxed yet stylish restaurant in Tonbridge.

The pair travelled the world with their careers, training and cooking in five star hotels including the Mandarin Oriental and the Radisson. Five countries and a Roux scholarship later, the talented chefs brought everything they had learned together to set up the restaurant. Dinesh is the manager, owner and pastry chef and Daya is his main chef, playing to their individual strengths and backgrounds.

They chose Kent because it's close enough to London, where they both still live, for them to travel every day and they love the countryside and its friendly towns. Gurkha Planet has been described as a hidden gem, tucked away down a side street in Tonbridge, but is recognised nationally for the quality of its food. In 2017 the restaurant scooped wins at both the British Curry Awards and the Asian Curry Awards, which joined an impressive line-up of its chefs' gold and silver medals!

There's also a very well established catering side to Gurkha Planet; Daya and Dinesh have prepared afternoon tea for Kenwood House and also produce bespoke food and drink for individuals. Though the focus is on Indian and Nepalese dishes in the restaurant, the catering can be done in any style according to the customer's preferences.

The à la carte menu features popular specials such as Thai green curry, fusion dishes that marry local produce — such as lamb reared on a farm in Tunbridge Wells — and unique festival creations that take inspiration from different regions of Nepal, which is where the name stems from; Gurkha means someone of Nepalese nationality and planet hints at the way they mingle Nepal's food with other culinary influences. The two chefs are passionate about the food they create at Gurkha Planet, and enjoy surprising and delighting customers with their fusion of cuisines and ingredients from around the world.

Preparation time: 15 minutes | Cooking time: 20 minutes | Serves: 1

# GURKHA PLANET

## NAVA RATNA CHARGRILLED PRAWNS

I love to infuse European food with Nepalese spices. This dish is a combination of Tibetan, European and Nepalese cuisine, so you have chargrilled prawns – a very Mediterranean dish – marinated in a Nepalese spice blend, and accompanied by taro or 'yam chilli' which is common in Nepalese and Tibetan cooking.

## INGREDIENTS

**For the nava ratna (9 spice mix):**

Pinch of ground cumin, ground coriander, chilli powder, Szechuan pepper, crushed black pepper, fenugreek powder, fennel seeds and salt

Dash of mustard oil and lemon juice

3g each garlic and ginger paste

**For the prawns:**

130g king prawns

80g taro

30g red, green and yellow pepper, diced into 2½ cm pieces

10g onion, sliced

15g pak choi

5 curry leaves

Salt and pepper

Pinch of green chilli, to taste

5g tomato ketchup

Dash of soy sauce, to taste

10g fresh tomato, diced

5g spring onion, roughly chopped

## METHOD

Combine all the ingredients for the nava ratna and thoroughly coat the prawns in the marinade. Cover with cling film and leave to marinate for 30 minutes. Chargrill the prawns until just cooked; you should see the flesh turning pink but make sure they don't become hard and rubbery.

Meanwhile, boil the taro as you would a potato, then peel the skin and dice the flesh. Heat a little oil in a pan and sauté the peppers, onion, and pak choi with the curry leaf. Then add salt, pepper and green chilli, followed by the ketchup, soy sauce, diced taro and tomato. Cook on a medium heat for about 1 minute, adding a little bit of water if needed to steam the vegetables slightly. Don't overcook the peppers, onion and pak choi as they must be crunchy. Finish by adding the chopped spring onion to the mixture, transferring it to a serving plate and topping with the chargrilled prawns.

# LIFE IS WHAT YOU BAKE IT

Jane Beedle was a finalist in the 2016 series of The Great British Bake Off and has since got involved with lots of food-related events around Kent, including Tree of Hope's Dine & Donate campaign.

Baking has always been a big part of Jane Beedle's life, way before she took part in The Great British Bake Off and reached the 2016 finals with her flair for classic cakes, biscuits and pastry. Her grandfather owned a bakery in Hastings, where Jane grew up, and the family connection was passed on by her dad who would always bring cakes and treats home for birthdays and occasions throughout her childhood. Jane stayed in the area, studying at the University of Kent and later bringing up her own family as well as running her garden design business in the beautiful Kentish countryside. "Living out here is like being on holiday," she says, "and I had no idea how foodie Kent really was until I discovered the rich pocket of producers, and even vineyards, that we're surrounded by."

Jane now balances running her own company with collaborations and events alongside some of those producers. That was what led to her involvement with Tree of Hope, as she met some of the team at a charity event and learnt about their Dine & Donate campaign. Jane was impressed by the concept, which not only allowed people to have a fantastic time enjoying a meal cooked by top local chefs, but encouraged generous contributions to the charity's work in a much more interactive way than simply sending in donations. It benefitted the community as well as the charity, and provided all kinds of opportunities to celebrate Kent's delicious food and drink, from the raffle at the launch in January 2018 – which featured a cake made especially by Jane – to showcasing the talents of the people who were involved.

There will be plenty more on the horizon for Jane both in terms of charity work and baking; she's keen to stay involved with Tree of Hope and spend more time supporting them. "Their expertise in organising and supporting individual campaigns for children all over the country is incredible; every penny donated to Tree of Hope is used exactly how you'd want it to be." Jane also looks forward to more demonstrations at food festivals and shows – which she says have woken up her inner show-off – and continuing to enjoy the unexpected and rewarding opportunities her baking journey presents!

Preparation time: 10 minutes, plus freezing | Serves: 12

# Jane Beedle

# EASY-PEASY ICE CREAM

Ice cream can be a bit of a bother to make, especially if you don't have an ice cream maker, but this recipe could change your mind. No custard making, no churning and no taking it out of the freezer every couple of hours to break up the ice crystals. Give it a go!

## INGREDIENTS

397g tin of condensed milk

300ml double cream

300ml Greek yoghurt (not low fat, it should have a creamy consistency)

1 tsp vanilla bean paste or vanilla extract

**For a lemon curd ice cream:**

1 jar (320g) of good quality or homemade lemon curd

**For a blackcurrant ice cream:**

400g frozen blackcurrants

50g caster sugar

## METHOD

Place all the ingredients into a bowl and whisk until the mixture thickens and lightly holds its shape. Place in a container suitable for the freezer and freeze. It's as simple as that!

Remove from the freezer 15 to 30 minutes before required so it softens and is easy to serve.

**Variations**

**For a lemon curd ice cream**

1 jar (320g) of good quality or homemade lemon curd.

Once the basic ice cream mixture has thickened, beat in half of the lemon curd. Place the mixture in a freezer container and swirl through the remainder of the curd so you can see ripples of lemon, then freeze and serve as above.

**For a blackcurrant ice cream**

Place the blackcurrants into a saucepan with the sugar and a splash of water, then heat gently until the blackcurrants are just defrosted. Do not boil or overheat as you want them to be cold when you add them to the mixture. Mash the berries and whisk into the ice cream mixture. Freeze.

If you can't find blackcurrants in the supermarket you can buy British ones online. I always keep a bag in the freezer. You could use raspberries instead, but I would sieve the fruit mixture to remove the pips and check how sweet they are to see if you need less sugar.

**For a Nutella, peanut butter or salted caramel ice cream**

Simply whisk your chosen addition into the mixture to taste. Easy-peasy and delicious.

**For a chocolate bar ice cream**

Try mashing up a Crunchie or a Bounty and stirring it into the ice cream mixture before freezing. Really, anything goes!

Preparation time: 20 minutes, plus chilling | Cooking time: approx. 1 hour 40 minutes | Serves: 8-10

# Jane Beedle

## APRICOT BAKEWELL

I love the tangy sweetness of apricots. They are delicious in midsummer eaten straight from the fruit bowl, but if you have some under ripe ones and don't want to wait until they are ready, then give this recipe a try. You can use tinned apricots if they're out of season, so this is a dessert to enjoy all year round.

### INGREDIENTS

**For the pastry:**
100g salted butter, softened
1 large egg yolk
½ tsp almond extract (optional)
75g icing sugar
160g plain flour

**For the filling:**
8-10 fresh apricots
190g caster sugar
130g salted butter, softened
2 large eggs
100g ground almonds
40g self-raising flour
½ tsp almond extract
40g amaretti biscuits (the crunchy ones)
30g flaked almonds

**To finish:**
2-3 tbsp apricot jam

### METHOD

Grease a 20cm loose-bottomed sandwich tin and preheat the oven to 180°c for fan, or 200°c for conventional.

**For the pastry**

Beat the softened butter and egg yolk together until light and fluffy, then add the almond extract if using and beat in the icing sugar. Fold in the plain flour until the mixture comes together then wrap the pastry in cling film and place in the fridge for 30 minutes.

**For the filling**

Place the apricots in a bowl and cover with boiling water. Leave for 5 minutes or longer if the apricots are very under ripe. Drain and then peel the apricots; the skins should now come off easily. Halve the fruit and remove the stones. Set aside seven halves. Roughly chop the rest of the apricots and place in a small saucepan with 60g of the caster sugar. Gently bring to the boil and simmer until syrupy. Mash them up roughly with a fork and set aside.

Roll out the chilled pastry and line the prepared tin, patching up any holes with spare pastry (it does tend to crack) and ensuring you have an even layer. Prick the bottom with a fork and trim the edges. Chill the pastry case for 15 minutes, then line it with baking parchment and fill with baking beans, bake in the preheated oven for 15 minutes, remove the parchment and beans and pop back in the oven for a further 5 minutes until dry and lightly coloured.

Reduce the oven temperature to 165°c for fan, 185°c for conventional. Place the softened butter, remaining sugar, eggs, ground almonds, flour and almond extract in a bowl and beat until combined. Spread the cooked apricots over the bottom of the pastry case. Crumble in the crunchy amaretti biscuits and then fill with the almond mixture, ensuring that the base is completely covered. Place the reserved apricot halves on the top and sprinkle over the flaked almonds, avoiding the apricots. Wrap some foil around the edges of the tin to prevent the pastry from overbrowning.

Place in the preheated oven and bake for approximately 45 minutes to 1 hour, or until the filling has set and a toothpick inserted into the middle comes out clean.

**To finish**

Heat the apricot jam with two tablespoons of water and brush the top of the apricots with the mixture. You can brush the whole top if you fancy, but I like the apricots shining out. Leave to cool before removing from the tin and serving.

Preparation time: 20 minutes, plus cooling | Cooking time: approx. 1 hour 15 minutes | Serves: 10-12

# Jane Beedle

# APPLE AND PECAN CRUMBLE CAKE WITH FUDGE SAUCE TOPPING

This is one of my favourite cakes to eat. It's packed full of delicious things and a real crowd pleaser, especially if, like me, you are not a huge fan of super sweet buttercream. The fudge sauce is a bit of an indulgence but hard to resist!

## INGREDIENTS

**For the cake:**
200g salted butter, softened
200g light muscovado sugar
3 large eggs, lightly beaten
350g self-raising flour
1 tsp baking powder
1 tsp cinnamon
250g cooking apples, peeled and diced
70g pecans, chopped

**For the crumble topping:**
50g plain flour
25g salted butter
25g light muscovado sugar
30g pecan nuts, chopped

**For the fudge sauce:**
75g salted butter
90g soft light brown sugar
150ml double cream

## METHOD

Grease a 20cm loose-bottomed cake tin and line the base. Preheat the oven to 160°c fan, or 180°c for a conventional oven.

**For the cake**

Cream together the butter and sugar until light and fluffy, then beat in the eggs a little at a time. Sift together the flour, baking powder and cinnamon and fold into the mixture. Fold in the diced apple and chopped pecans. Spoon the mixture into the prepared tin and level off.

**For the crumble topping**

Make the crumble topping by rubbing the butter into the flour until the mixture resembles fine breadcrumbs. Stir in the sugar and nuts until evenly combined. Sprinkle the crumble topping evenly over the cake mixture.

Pop the cake into the preheated oven and bake for approximately 1 hour to 1 hour 15 minutes until a skewer inserted into the centre comes out clean. Leave to cool in the tin for 10 to 15 minutes, then remove from the tin and place on a wire rack to cool completely. Meanwhile, make the fudge sauce.

**For the fudge sauce**

Place all the ingredients into a saucepan and heat gently until the sugar has melted. Bring the mixture up to a vigorous boil and cook for about 3 to 4 minutes, keep an eye on it to ensure it doesn't burn. Remove from the heat and set aside.

**To serve**

When the cake has cooled, place on a nice serving plate or cake stand, drizzle the fudge sauce over the top and let a little run down the sides and onto the plate. How much you use is up to you, but you don't want to completely cover the delicious crumble topping. Any leftover sauce can be stored in a jar and eaten with ice cream or, if you are like me, by the spoonful when you spot it in the fridge. Either way, I can promise you it won't hang about for long!

# A ZEST FOR FLAVOUR

Food, drink and travel with a citrus twist…

Inspired by Mediterranean flavours and textures, The Lemon Grove is run by Bruce McMichael, a food writer, communicator and cooking demonstrator. It's a website and blog that covers all things food, drink and travel 'for those of us who never stop exploring with our taste buds and passports'. Bruce is also an experienced photographer and author, having provided the visual feasts on his website since it began. He has written two books based on his own experiences in business, the first of which, Cook Wrap Sell, is a popular how-to guide to setting up successful, home-based food businesses. The follow up title, Cook Wrap Export, is about food producers selling internationally.

Closer to home, Bruce is always keen to support small independents and promote the food scene across Kent, particularly in Tunbridge Wells where he has made his home. In keeping with his website's theme, Bruce has developed a range of citrus-based sauces and chutneys with a local chef who makes the products with fresh fruits and vegetables, many of which are sourced from Kent's own countryside. The Lemon and Ginger Sauce, Lemon and Lime Marmalade, Plum and Lime Relish, and Orange Curry Chutney are bottled and then sold by Bruce at farmers' markets across the county. He also does cookery demonstrations at food festivals and similar events using seasonal ingredients and, of course, citrus fruits to show how versatile and exciting they can be.

Innovative and delicious ways to use his favourite flavours are never far from Bruce's mind. This skill and passion shone through on the 2017 TV cookery competition, Gordon Ramsay's Culinary Genius, on which Bruce was a winning contestant. He took his children on holiday to Sicily with the prize money, where the family could enjoy – you guessed it! – some of the tastiest citrus fruits right off the tree. Combining his love of good food and drink with travel has taken Bruce to many exciting new places; he has written for publications across Kent and is a member of the Guild of Food Writers and also of Slow Food International, an organisation focused on preserving local traditions and supporting artisan, small-scale farmers.

Looking to the future, The Lemon Grove will host more podcasts and video food stories, which will feature book reviews and cooking demonstrations. These will run alongside the variety of regular posts, plus Bruce's visits and appearances on the culinary scene around the county, keeping Kent's foodies up to date and informed by an eclectic collection of tastes and talents.

Preparation time: 25 minutes | Cooking time: 35 minutes | Serves: 4

# The Lemon Grove

## ONE POT LAMB CUTLETS WITH LEMON & ROSEMARY

This tasty Mediterranean-inspired one pot dinner showcases tasty lamb cutlets flavoured with lemon and rosemary and served on a bed of new potatoes, peppers, olives and capers.

## INGREDIENTS

4 lemons

2 tbsp olive oil

1 large clove of garlic, crushed

6 rosemary sprigs, leaves picked from 4 and chopped

2 anchovies, roughly chopped

Salt and pepper

or 150ml Lemon & Ginger Sauce from The Lemon Grove

8 lamb cutlets, trimmed of excess fat

500g new potatoes, washed (no need to peel) and thinly sliced

2 red peppers, deseeded and thickly sliced

6 small vine tomatoes, halved

50g black olives, pitted and chopped

3 tbsp capers, drained and rinsed

10 Kentish cobnuts, dry roasted in a frying pan and crushed (optional)

2 tbsp chopped soft herbs (mint, coriander, parsley etc.)

## METHOD

Zest and juice one and a half of the lemons, then slice the other half and set aside. Whisk the lemon zest and juice with 1 tablespoon of the olive oil, the clove of garlic, chopped rosemary leaves, anchovies (for an umami flavour boost) and seasoning.

Swirl the trimmed lamb cutlets into the marinade or lemon and ginger sauce, which makes a great alternative. Toss to coat, then leave to marinate for at least 30 minutes. Preheat the oven to 220°c.

Toss the potatoes with half a tablespoon of olive oil and some seasoning. Tip into a large, shallow roasting dish and put in the hot oven for 15 minutes. Shake the dish to loosen the potatoes then top with the peppers, sliced half lemon, remaining rosemary sprigs and tomatoes. Drizzle with the remaining olive oil and season. Return to the oven for a further 10 minutes.

Place the marinated lamb cutlets on top of the veg. Scatter over the olives, capers and the cobnuts for extra crunch, if using. Cook for a final 15 minutes, turning the lamb halfway through. It should be just pink when done.

**To finish**

Halve the remaining two lemons and char under the grill for 2 minutes or until the flesh is lightly burnt. Place one half on each portion and sprinkle the chopped herbs over the finished dish just before serving.

For added theatre, serve from the roasting dish with a side such as Dijon mustard glazed carrots and perhaps a dollop or two of mint sauce, or apple and mint jelly. To make the Dijon mustard glazed carrots, clean and steam 750g of carrots until tender – the small Chantenay variety are tasty – and at the same time, put two teaspoons of light brown soft sugar and 15g of salted butter in a large pan. Heat until melted, stir in two teaspoons of Dijon mustard, then add the carrots. Tumble with some chopped parsley or spring onions and serve hot.

# LOOKING GOOD ON PAPER

In April 2017 the Papermakers Arms became a free house for the first time in its history; the new owner's contemporary spin on a cosy country pub has brought its legacy right up to date.

---

Graham Perrin took on the lease of the Papermakers Arms in 2011, and was delighted to take up the opportunity to purchase the pub six years later. Since its new lease of life as a free house for the first time in the pub's history, the century-old watering hole has seen a few changes that have brought out its character and given it a local reputation for great food and drink. Based in the pretty village of Plaxtol, a hidden gem not far from the hustle and bustle of Sevenoaks and Tonbridge, the Papermakers Arms benefits from a great location in the beautiful Kentish countryside.

Each member of the team that Graham has brought together plays a role in making the most of the community around them, and giving back in equal measure. Rachel, the front of house manager, ensures a warm welcome for locals and visitors alike, while chef Tim likes to create new dishes from produce that's grown or reared within a 5 minute drive radius for the most part! The menu is a nod to traditional pub grub but with a much more refined edge, plus inspiration from cuisines all over the world including

Tim's home nation, South Africa. The Sunday roast has been especially popular, showcasing a choice of meat from Coldbreath family butchers' own farm in Ightham. "We've built some great relationships within the area, not just in terms of suppliers but with our customers as well," says marketing manager Julie, who's always looking for more ways to bring the pub back to its roots.

The Papermakers Arms was built in 1900, though it had existed since the 1800s on a different site nearby. The original pub catered for the local paper mill workers and was initially licensed just to sell beer. Not everything has changed since then; guests will still find a tempting selection of beverages, including different guest beers every week from across the UK, and closer to home the apple juice on the menu comes from Plaxtol's own trees! Keeping its history and community alive while putting a contemporary take on good food, good drinks and a great atmosphere are the hallmarks of the Papermakers Arms, which the team generally agree is "just lots of fun to work at!"

Preparation time: 30 minutes | Cooking time: 40 minutes | Serves: 6

# PAPERMAKERS ARMS
# LAMB BOBOTIE

Bobotie (ba-boor-tea) is a delicious mix of spiced meat and fruits with an egg-based topping and is a very popular South African dish. This dish brings back fond memories as a kid growing up in South Africa and I'd have it as often as I could! Bobotie is traditionally made with minced beef and you can try an alternative version by swapping the lamb for beef. I also like to add a bit of veg to my rice for extra flavour.

## INGREDIENTS

**For the bobotie:**

1 large white onion, diced

Splash of olive oil

4 cloves of garlic, chopped

1.5kg minced leg of lamb

3 tsp turmeric

2 tsp madras curry powder

2 tsp ground cumin

2 tsp ground coriander

150g mango chutney

½ tsp each of salt and pepper

**For the savoury custard:**

4 eggs

250ml milk

1 tsp turmeric

½ tsp each of salt and pepper

2 bay leaves

**For the yellow rice:**

2 tsp turmeric

350g basmati rice

1 red pepper, diced

1 courgette, diced

1 red onion, diced

150g peas

2 tbsp olive oil

½ tsp each of salt and pepper

**To serve:**

Bunch of watercress

## METHOD

Preheat the oven to 200°c (180°c in a fan oven). Sauté the onion in a little oil until brown, then add the garlic and cook for 1 minute. Add the lamb and cook until browned off; about 5 to 8 minutes. Add all of the spices, chutney, salt and pepper and mix together until well combined.

Line a 20cm square loaf tin (ours is 9cm deep) with greaseproof parchment paper and press the bobotie mixture firmly down into the dish.

**For the savoury custard**

Beat the eggs then add the milk, turmeric, salt and pepper. Mix well. Pour the custard on top of the lamb mixture and put the bay leaves on top. Bake in the preheated oven for 20 to 30 minutes, or until the custard has set and is firm to the touch.

**For the yellow rice**

Bring 450ml of water to the boil, add the turmeric and rice and cook for 15 to 18 minutes. Sauté the red pepper, courgette, red onion and peas in the olive oil for 6 to 8 minutes; they should still have a little bite. Drain the rice and leave to stand for 2 to 3 minutes then stir through the cooked vegetables and season with salt and pepper.

**To serve**

Cut the bobotie into six portions and plate up with some of the yellow rice. We use a rice mould but you could also use a dome shaped coffee cup. Add a final flourish with a small bunch of watercress and enjoy!

# Something Old, Something New

Strong values and high standards are at the forefront of The Plough at Ivy Hatch's rejuvenation into a cherished local, and a country pub that does things just a little differently.

April 2018 marked the emergence of something both new and old in the village of Ivy Hatch. Business partners Dale and James had always worked in hospitality, more recently running a café and then catering in the area. James grew up in Kent and The Plough used to be his local, so when the pair saw it come up for sale, looking a bit sad and run down, it seemed like a great opportunity to recreate a much-loved country pub. Their restoration aimed to fulfil The Plough's role in the community, but also to offer something a little different that was interesting, informal, and exciting.

The ethos is reflected in all aspects of the pub, from the interior to the menus. The range of dishes is available to choose from all day and comprises small and big plates that you can combine for any meal. The lion's share of the menu features pub classics, but these are blended with little twists and new inventions from Alan, Dan, and their experienced head chef Dominic. "There's no distinct style when it comes to our food," says Dale, "it's more of a fusion of things we like that evolves as we go along." Pairing a meal with high quality drinks is just as important to Dale and James, so they've curated a selection of craft beer and natural wines from smaller, mostly independent producers across the UK and Europe. Natural wines are made with as little intervention as possible, giving them a distinct taste that's different to most.

There are several spaces, each with a character of its own, throughout the pub where guests can enjoy a drink and a bite to eat. The conservatory, outdoor seating and large beer garden (currently in development but already populated by the pub's own chickens and a vegetable patch!) are great for summer, then there's a snug and cosy bar which provide warmth on a winter evening. Rather than describe The Plough as a restaurant, Dale and James want to establish their venture as "everyone's favourite local" which means focusing on making their country pub setting really friendly and welcoming for all.

Preparation time: 1 hour | Cooking time: 3-4 hours | Serves: 4

# The Plough at Ivy Hatch

## CHILLI OX CHEEK RAMEN

This Asian dish was inspired by a love of far eastern cuisine with simplicity in mind, to create something that with a small amount of work is delicious and versatile. Beef cheeks, if not easily obtainable, can be substituted with another slow cooked meat, such as brisket or shin of beef.

### INGREDIENTS

Glug of oil
4 350g trimmed beef cheeks
100g ginger
4 cloves of garlic
70g chilli paste
1-2 fresh red chillies
4 tbsp light soy sauce
2 sticks of lemongrass
4 kaffir lime leaves
1.5 litres good quality beef stock
1 packet of rice noodles
500g tenderstem broccoli
Maldon sea salt and cracked black pepper
2 carrots
1 red cabbage
Bunch of coriander
4 eggs

### METHOD

Preheat the oven to 150°c. Next take a casserole dish or pot that can be transferred to the oven easily from the stove. Heat this pan up with some oil and season the cheeks well. Sear the cheeks in the hot pan, turning on all sides until well browned, then take the cheeks out and set aside.

Put the pan back on the heat and add the ginger and garlic. Fry until fragrant, add in the chilli paste and stir for a few seconds. Throw in some roughly sliced fresh chillies if you like it extra hot at this point. Place the beef cheeks back in the pan, add the soy sauce and coat the meat thoroughly. Split the lemongrass down the middle and put into the pan along with the kaffir lime leaves. Add the beef stock and bring to the boil. Cover and place in the oven for at least 3 hours 30 minutes. Check to make sure it's tender and falling apart to the touch. If a knife doesn't go through with ease, cover and put back into the oven for 15 to 20 minutes then check again.

Prepare the rice noodles according to packet instructions; alternatively heat them in sesame oil. Blanche the broccoli, or cook until just al dente then griddle on all sides to add char marks and a smoky flavour. Season with Maldon sea salt and cracked black pepper. Peel the carrots then create ribbons of it with the peeler. Finely slice the cabbage, as thinly as possible. Roughly chop the coriander, and finely slice the remaining red chilli.

Make sure the eggs are at room temperature, then place into a pan of boiling water for around 5 minutes 30 seconds and then plunge into bowl of ice water to stop the cooking, then peel after a couple of minutes.

**To serve**

To assemble the dish, place the raw carrot, broccoli and cabbage on one side of the bowl. Place the noodles in the centre and a beef cheek on the other side. Pass the braising liquid through a fine sieve into a saucepan and heat though. You can leave the stock to reduce for a more intense flavour, and check the seasoning to adjust if needed. Pour the finished broth into the bowl and top with one egg, some coriander and chilli, then enjoy.

# CULINARY POETRY

The Poet at Matfield is all about offering a dining experience that stands out from the crowd, from inventive food and drink to events and occasions.

Describing The Poet at Matfield as a pub with restaurant in the heart of Kent belies what is unique about the warm and inviting venue. It's co-owned and managed by four business partners, who took it over in February 2016 and made it totally theirs. Andy Urbanek is one of these four and also heads up the front of house team. He ensures that the friendly welcome customers are greeted with sets the tone for their whole visit. "Our focus is on our customers," says Andy, "so all our energies both front of house and in the kitchen go towards making sure they have a great time."

Petrus Madutlela is The Poet's head chef and co-owner, and he pours inspiration from all over the world into the dishes. Over the summer this means cooking up braai – South African barbecue – so Petrus can showcase the fantastic classics from his home country, including Boerewors sausages, chicken wings, pulled pork chakalaka and much more. The daily a la carte and tasting menus are no less diverse, featuring food based on traditional British cuisine with an inventive twist and above all, emphasis on making

everything enjoyable to eat. "We cook as we feel," says Petrus. Fresh produce is crucial to this approach, so most of The Poet's suppliers are based in Kent, supplemented by herbs grown in the pub's own garden.

The outdoor space is a perfect spot for enjoying braai and the annual gin festival, while indoors there are three areas for casual dining and a well-stocked bar. The traditional décor and little touches to the table settings give the pub a warm and homely feel whatever the weather, and there's a small room which can be hired out for occasions and celebrations. In 2017 The Poet was awarded Best Destination Pub in Kent by Muddy Stilettos, which the team were all really proud to receive. Chris and Debbie Salter, the pub's other owners, are both devout foodies and like to be actively involved with all aspects of the business. "We are very proud of what the four of us have created together to date and will try to keep improving on everything we do at The Poet to create the best environment we can for our customers to enjoy."

Preparation time: 10 minutes | Serves: 1

# The Poet at Matfield

## M & H LEMON ELDERFLOWER

To make this lovely light and refreshing cocktail, you will need a martini glass, a Boston shaker, a hawthorn strainer and a fine strainer such as one used for tea leaves. It was created to celebrate Meghan and Harry's wedding on the theme of their lemon and elderflower wedding cake.

## INGREDIENTS

½ lemon, juiced (about 25ml)

20ml sugar syrup

60ml elderflower gin liqueur
(we use Edinburgh Distillery)

1 egg white (about 50ml)

**To garnish:**

Sprigs of fresh mint

Fresh elderflowers

## METHOD

Chill the martini glass and pour the lemon juice, sugar syrup and gin liqueur into your shaker then add the egg white. Close the shaker and dry shake, not too hard, for around 8 seconds. Carefully open the shaker and add ice until the shaker is two thirds full. Close the shaker and shake fast for around 15 seconds.

Have the chilled glass ready. It doesn't need any ice. Open the shaker and taste the cocktail to check the flavour is balanced. Double strain the contents with the hawthorn strainer on top of the shaker and the fine strainer above the glass to catch any ice shards.

Garnish the cocktail with a little sprig of fresh mint, and a few fresh elderflowers if they are in season. Enjoy!

Preparation time: 15 minutes | Cooking time: 5 minutes | Serves: 4 as a starter or 2 as a main

# THE POET AT MATFIELD

## TUNA TATAKI WITH MISO MAYONNAISE

Tataki is a Japanese method of cooking. This tuna tataki recipe is simple, super healthy and packed with punchy flavours. Ask your fishmonger for the freshest possible yellow fin tuna for best results.

## INGREDIENTS

**For the tuna tataki:**

3 tbsp soy sauce

1 tbsp Japanese rice vinegar

1 tbsp fish sauce

1 tsp caster sugar

1 lemon, juiced

1 spring onion, thinly sliced

20g fresh ginger, finely shredded

1 red chilli, deseeded and finely chopped (optional)

2 tbsp sesame oil

400g yellow fin tuna (look for the MSC logo if possible)

Salt and black pepper

**For the miso mayonnaise:**

80g mayonnaise

40g light miso paste

1 tbsp soy sauce

**To serve:**

1 nashi (Asian) pear, thinly sliced

Handful of hazelnuts, toasted and chopped

## METHOD

**For the tuna tataki**

Combine the soy sauce, Japanese rice vinegar, fish sauce, caster sugar and lemon juice in a small saucepan. Bring to the boil, remove from the heat and allow to cool. Once cooled, add the spring onion, ginger and chilli if using. Whisk together and keep the sauce at room temperature.

Heat the sesame oil in a non-stick pan over a high heat until very hot. Season the tuna to taste with salt and ground black pepper before carefully adding it to the hot pan. Sear for 10 seconds on each side, then transfer the cooked tuna onto a clean chopping board to rest for a few minutes. Cut the tuna into 2cm cubes and place in a bowl. Add the tataki sauce and mix gently. Leave to marinate for a couple of minutes while you make the mayonnaise.

**For the miso mayonnaise**

In a small bowl, combine all three ingredients until smooth and check the taste.

**To serve**

Divide the tuna between serving plates, arrange the slices of nashi pear on top, and finish with a dollop or drizzle of mayo and a sprinkle of the toasted hazelnuts.

Preparation time: 10 minutes | Cooking time: approx. 25 minutes | Serves: 2

# The Poet at Matfield

## CEP MUSHROOM FREGOLA WITH POACHED HEN'S EGG

Fregola is a variety of pasta from Sardinia which resembles giant couscous. It's perfect for soaking up flavours. In this recipe I've used a similar method to risotto, combining the pasta with flavourful ceps (porcini mushrooms), fresh sage and a creamy poached hen's egg which dresses the dish.

### INGREDIENTS

150g fregola

Salt and pepper

1 tbsp olive oil

25g butter

6 cep (porcini) mushrooms, cleaned and sliced

2 cloves of garlic, peeled and chopped

1 sprig of rosemary, leaves finely chopped

4 sage leaves, thinly sliced

2 large fresh hen's eggs

1 tsp white wine or malt vinegar

The ceps can be replaced with 2 large Portobello mushrooms, and the fregola can be replaced with giant couscous if either is hard to get hold of.

**For the Parmesan crisp:**

160g Parmesan, grated

### METHOD

Cook the fregola in a pan of seasoned boiling water for around 10 minutes, until tender and slightly chewy. Drain and return to the pan. Stir in a little olive oil to prevent sticking.

Heat the butter in a non-stick frying pan over medium-low heat. Add the mushrooms and sauté until lightly golden. Add the garlic and rosemary, and season well with salt. After a couple of minutes add the sliced sage leaves to finish.

Add the mushroom mixture to the pan of fregola and toss lightly. Season with freshly ground pepper to taste.

Finally, poach the eggs. Half fill a large saucepan with water and bring to the boil. Season with salt, and add the vinegar. Crack the first egg into a cup. Stir the water rapidly with a balloon whisk, then pour the egg into the centre of the mini whirlpool you've created. Reduce the heat to low, and cook for exactly 4 minutes. Remove using a slotted spoon and drain on kitchen paper. Repeat for the second egg.

**For the Parmesan crisp**

Spread the grated Parmesan out on a non-stick ovenproof mat or tray lined with greaseproof paper. Bake at 180°c for approximately 8 minutes, until golden and crisp. Slide off the mat or tray carefully before serving.

**To serve**

Divide the mushroom fregola into two bowls and top each with a poached egg. Place the Parmesan crisp over the dish and serve immediately.

# WE'LL MEET AGAIN

Tunbridge Wells is home to Rendez-Vous, a brasserie with French influences that marries local ingredients with a fresh approach to a classic cuisine.

Rendez-Vous is a restaurant with a style all of its own, created by Mark Harper and his small team of family and close friends. As a professional chef, Mark had opened a restaurant called Le Rendezvous with his French business partner, but decided it was time to branch out into his own project when the opportunity arose to buy his business partner's other venue. Mark redeveloped the restaurant into Rendez-Vous, which he describes as a brasserie with French influences. He didn't want to go down the same route of classic French cuisine, but as his wife Lydie is French there are some touches that echo those flavours and styles.

A big part of the menu is comprised of game, which is all from the countryside around Tunbridge Wells and is prepared from plucking to roasting at the restaurant. When it's in season, Mark and his chef John have venison every other week, and are genuinely enthusiastic about having so much local produce to work with. "That's the luxury of being on the Kent-Sussex border," says Mark, "as everything we want is here, from fish to meat to veg, so we don't have to travel far for our food."

Many of the dishes are real favourites with the regular customers, and the most popular remain on the menu year round alongside an ever-evolving specials board, plus some inventions from Mark and John, that have even included a few wacky ice cream flavours by request! They love being able to invent things that keep everyone – from the staff to the diners – interested and coming back for more. Everything is homemade and the friendly faces on both sides give the bistro style environment a homely and welcoming feel. "We're well supported by the locals," Mark says, "and it's really nice that even our two children can join us in the restaurant on Saturdays when Lydie and I are here together."

Rendez-Vous is led by the best of Kent and Sussex produce, and driven by the commitment to a strong vision for the restaurant that Mark has cultivated in collaboration with his close-knit team. The joy for them stems from the freedom that owning and running a small, family business affords, and remaining a part of this individual set up is something they all look forward to continuing.

Preparation time: 30 minutes | Cooking time: 1 hour 50 minutes | Serves: 12

# RENDEZ-VOUS

# WARM GINGER PUDDING WITH CARAMEL SAUCE AND HONEYCOMB ICE CREAM

"This recipe has been with me for nearly 30 years. It was passed down to me by a very good chef de partie who assisted in my training when I was an apprentice at Boodles in London. The beauty of it is that if you exchange half of the golden syrup for treacle you have a very fine gingerbread. So it's about time I shared it and I hope you enjoy making it as much as I do."
John Boreham, head chef.

## INGREDIENTS

**For the ginger pudding:**
454g golden syrup
227g butter
113g granulated sugar
284ml milk
2 eggs
454g plain flour
4 tsp baking powder
56g ground ginger

**For the caramel sauce:**
500g granulated sugar
250g unsalted butter
568ml double cream

**For the honeycomb:**
250g granulated sugar
75g local honey
1tsp bicarbonate of soda

**For the honeycomb ice cream:**
1.136l milk
454g granulated sugar
10 egg yolks
568ml double cream

## METHOD

**For the ginger pudding**

Preheat the oven to 160 to 170°c. Line a medium-sized deep baking tray with foil or parchment and then grease lightly. Place the golden syrup, butter and sugar in a pan and gently heat until sugar has dissolved, then leave to cool. Once the mixture has cooled (about 5 minutes) add the milk and eggs, thoroughly combine, then fold in the flour, baking powder and ground ginger. Mix well and then pass the cake batter through a conical strainer into the prepared baking tray. Bake the pudding in the preheated oven for 20 minutes, then cover the top with foil to prevent burning and bake for a further 90 minutes or until a thin knife inserted into the centre comes out clean. Let the cake cool and then cut into 12 equal pieces.

**For the caramel sauce**

Heat the sugar in a clean pan until caramelisation (around 190°c) then add the butter. Once melted, add the cream and simmer the sauce for 10 minutes. Remove from the heat and serve.

**For the honeycomb**

Heat the sugar and honey to exactly 170°c then take the pan off the heat and whisk in the bicarbonate of soda. Quickly pour the mixture onto a sheet of baking parchment and allow to cool until solid. Break into bite-sized pieces.

**For the honeycomb ice cream**

Bring the milk to the boil in a saucepan, then whisk in the sugar and egg yolks. Bring the mixture back to the boil, whisking rapidly, and then remove from the heat. Leave to cool and then transfer into an ice cream machine. Churn until a slushy consistency and then add the cream. Continue to churn until thick and creamy, adding the pieces of honeycomb at regular stages. Place in an ice cream container and freeze to -18°c.

**To serve**

Place a piece of warm ginger pudding onto a plate. Pour some warmed caramel sauce over the pudding. Serve with a generous scoop of honeycomb ice cream in a small ramekin on the side.

# A POP OF LOCAL FLAVOUR

Chef Russell Goad has brought exciting dining experiences to Kent with his supper clubs and pop-ups across the county.

Rustled Up is a new venture that brings together everything that's best about food and community, aptly named after the man in the driving seat, Russell Goad. He began branching out from his career as a professional chef in 2016, when it all started with a Christmas dinner held at his home to raise money for charity. That led to a couple more dinners which raised upwards of £2000 for charities in Kent, and when Russell saw that his hobby had escalated into hugely popular events catering for up to 50 people, he decided to start doing them for himself.

Following a break from the recipe development and teaching that comprised his day job, Russell travelled the world for a year and then came back to Kent ready to share his culinary inspirations with eager diners. Russell's style of cooking is all about flavour and keeping presentation appealing but simple, so everything on the plate has a need to be there. Though he doesn't restrict himself with seasonality and locality, they are the focal point of his cooking, and Russell enjoys sourcing his ingredients through Kent's many excellent suppliers. "There's such fantastic produce in this area," says Russell, "so I love to create dishes around a core ingredient that really stands out."

Cooking with home-grown fish, vegetables, meat and other delicacies is one way to connect with the community; another is to hold events for local people to enjoy again and again. Some of Rustled Up's most popular dining during 2018 has come in the form of supper clubs, most recently held in Tonbridge and sold out in a day! Word of mouth has brought more and more guests to Russell's evening events, including familiar faces that return each time with friends and friends of friends in tow. The six course tasting menu goes where Russell's inspiration takes it and is all prepared by the chef himself, with the invaluable help of his friend and fellow chef Leyli.

Russell hopes to continue his supper clubs alongside his next full time job, creating seasonal events simply for the love of cooking great food, to be enjoyed in a relaxed environment with no pretensions. His ethos runs through the whole venture and Russell would love to translate that into his own restaurant one day, as long as he can stay cooking in Kent!

Preparation time: 1 hour 15 minutes | Cooking time: 2 hours | Serves: 4

# RUSTLED UP

## DRESSED CRAB, TOMATO SALAD, CONSOMMÉ, SQUID INK CRACKER

This recipe brings together some of my favourite ingredients in a simple yet refined dish, showcasing fantastic British tomatoes at their best, with vibrant colour and intense flavour that pairs harmoniously with the sweet and salty crab. Perfect for a dinner party starter as the consommé and crackers can be prepared ahead of time, or simply enjoyed as I do, selfishly with a crisp glass of white!

## INGREDIENTS

**For the squid ink cracker:**
75g small tapioca pearls
450ml cold water
4g squid ink

**For the tomato consommé:**
550g ripe medium vine tomatoes
6 basil leaves
1 small clove of garlic, grated
2-3 tsp sherry vinegar
30ml gin
Generous pinch of Maldon sea salt
1 tsp freshly grated horseradish (optional)

**For the dressed crab:**
200g picked white crab
30g good quality mayonnaise
Few drops of lemon juice
Pinch of Maldon sea salt

**For the tomato salad:**
250g mixed heritage tomatoes (from the Isle of Wight if possible, as these are the best)
1 tsp extra-virgin olive oil
Pinch of Maldon sea salt

## METHOD

Preheat the oven to 80°c fan oven, or 100°c for a conventional.

**For the squid ink cracker**

Put the tapioca pearls and cold water into a saucepan over a medium heat and cook at a gentle simmer for around 15 to 20 minutes, or until the pearls begin to turn translucent, stirring every few minutes to prevent sticking. Drain the tapioca, tip the gloopy mixture into a bowl and carefully combine with the ink. Pour onto a flat baking tray lined with greaseproof paper and spread the pearls into one layer with a palette knife. Cook in the preheated oven for 1½ to 2 hours, until the mixture feels dry and peels easily off the paper. Remove paper and leave to cool.

Preheat a deep fat fryer or medium-sized pan with about 3cm of sunflower or rapeseed oil to 190°c. Break the tapioca sheet into pieces and carefully place into the hot oil one at a time. Within seconds they will float up, so gently push into the oil for a further few seconds until puffed, then place onto a tray lined with kitchen paper.

**For the tomato consommé**

Blend the tomatoes with the basil, a quarter of the garlic, two teaspoons of the vinegar, the gin, salt and horseradish if using on a high speed until smooth, taste the mixture for seasoning and add more garlic, salt, vinegar and gin to taste. Pour the mixture into a large bowl lined with muslin, carefully gather and tie the top then hang over the bowl, allowing the consommé to strain through the cloth. Leave for around 1 hour or until all the liquid has been strained. You should have about 400ml. Cover and refrigerate until 30 minutes before required.

**For the dressed crab**

Carefully mix the mayonnaise, lemon juice and a pinch of salt through the crab without breaking up large pieces. Add more lemon juice and salt to taste.

**For the tomato salad**

Remove the core from any larger tomatoes and cut into random bite-sized pieces. Just before serving, dress the tomatoes with the oil and sea salt.

**To serve**

Dividing everything between four small bowls, place a mound of the tomato salad on one side and the crab on the other. Carefully pour 30ml of the consommé down one side of the bowl, trying not to splash, and drizzle a few drops of extra-virgin olive oil around the consommé so it splits out. To finish, break the squid ink cracker into smaller pieces and dot around the bowl, then serve the dish with more crackers on the side.

# SEAFOOD AND EAT IT

Sankey's has something to offer every foodie with its Seafood Bar & Kitchen, fine dining restaurant The Old Fishmarket, and two award-winning fishmongers in Tunbridge Wells and Tonbridge.

Across each aspect of the Sankey's family business, one ethos brings it all together. This is the commitment to sourcing the best food and drink around, whether it's going to the fishmongers, the kitchen and bar, or the restaurant. "Produce is king," as owner Matthew Sankey says, "and being dependent on seasonality and the elements is a fantastic way of working – you're always changing and aiming for the best." His team talk to fishermen and market traders every day, and the end result is truly the freshest fish and seafood to be found.

Since their first foray into the food and beverage industry, Sankey's hospitality has always been food-led. In the 1960s Matthew's grandfather bought a pub, and the family have "never looked back" since. His father learnt the ropes too and then bought his own property in 1989. This was the site on Mount Ephraim, where Sankey's Seafood Kitchen & Bar is located today. Matthew bought out the business when his father retired, and has overseen its development into a thriving venture with four venues.

The Seafood Bar & Kitchen is a relaxed, informal eatery which puts craft beer side by side with interesting food from surf and turf to burgers. The menu and drinks offering has changed quite a bit over the years, but the team are still using the same crab and lobster supplier that Matthew's grandfather worked with. The majority of the fish and seafood comes directly from Sankey's own fishmongers. Well established in Tunbridge Wells, with a second site recently opened in Tonbridge, the fishmongers also supplies over 150 restaurants around Kent. It has professionals on hand to help shoppers choose and prepare anything from oysters to luxurious deli items, but also offers free home delivery for those wanting to buy online.

Last but definitely not least, The Old Fishmarket provides Kent's discerning diners with somewhere to indulge themselves and enjoy classic seafood dishes made with prime ingredients. Restaurant guests can see the chefs at work in the central open kitchen, and celebrate with champagne and Kent's own sparkling wines from the extensive wine list. Just like everything the latest generation of Sankey's hospitality turns its hand to, the restaurant creates a dining experience to remember with fresh fish and seafood as its star attraction.

Preparation time: 10 minutes | Cooking time: 35 minutes | Serves: 4

# SANKEY'S

# THE SANKEY'S SMOKIE

There is something about smoked haddock that nothing else can match; the succulent tanned flakes of smoky sweet fish are irresistible. This dish is by far the most popular item on the menu at The Seafood Kitchen & Bar on Mt Ephraim, and we can't seem to make enough of it, especially during the winter months.

## INGREDIENTS

500g natural smoked haddock, skinned and pin boned (keep the skin) – we can prepare this for you in our fishmongers

568ml (1 pint) full-fat milk

4 king prawns per person (optional)

2 bay leaves

1 sprig of thyme

1 tsp peppercorns

100g unsalted butter

100g plain flour

400g cheddar cheese, grated

4 handfuls of baby leaf spinach

4 free-range hens eggs (optional)

## METHOD

Pour the milk into a wide pan and add the bay leaves, thyme and peppercorns. Roll the fish skin into a tube to prevent it breaking up, lay the haddock into the milk and gently poach for about 5 minutes. You may also wish to add prawns to the dish at this stage; about four king prawns per person should be enough.

Next, make a roux by melting the butter in a saucepan, adding the flour bit by bit to make a paste and cook out for about 1 minute over a low heat. Carefully lift the haddock out of the milk and set aside. Strain the milk and then slowly add it to the flour and butter paste, stirring continuously to make a white sauce. Stir for around 5 to 10 minutes or until you get a nice even thick sauce. Add half of the grated cheese, stir in and then remove the pan from the heat.

In a baking dish (or you can do this in individual ovenproof bowls) layer the spinach on the bottom, then add the poached haddock, and prawns if using, before evenly pouring the sauce over the top. Coat with the remaining cheese and brown under a hot grill.

**To serve**

If you wish to top the smokie with a poached egg, poach the eggs while the dish is under the grill, then place an egg on top of each portion when you're ready to serve. Serve with nice crusty bread for dipping and mopping up the sauces.

Preparation time: 10 minutes | Cooking time: 15 minutes | Serves: 4

# SANKEY'S

## SPAGHETTI VONGOLE

Palourdes clams are just the sweetest little things, and just the right size for this dish.
You can use the cheaper Venus clams but they don't quite have the sweetness for this dish.
You can add razor clams if you really want to make an impact at a dinner party.

## INGREDIENTS

½ pack of dried spaghetti or linguine (our preferred brand is De Cecco)

1 clove of garlic, minced

1 banana shallot, diced

1 tbsp extra-virgin olive oil

1 fresh red chilli, chopped

500g Palourdes clams, washed well in cold water

1 glass of white wine

1 bunch of flat leaf parsley, chopped

Sea salt and cracked black pepper, to taste

## METHOD

Bring a large pot of salted water to the boil and cook the pasta according to the instructions on the pack. Meanwhile, sweat the garlic and shallot in the olive oil until softened but not browned and then add the fresh chilli. Add the clams then when the pan has come back up to temperature add the white wine and immediately cover. Once the clams begin to open, add the cooked pasta and chopped parsley. Toss gently using a pair of tongs and let everything get to know each other in the pan. Season to taste with sea salt and black pepper, then transfer into a nice large pasta dish and let everyone serve themselves at the table.

Preparation time: 10 minutes | Cooking time: 30 minutes | Serves: 2

# SANKEY'S

# A BANGING SIMPLE CURRY

This is a curry that I cook at home all the time, as you can play around with the ingredients to suit your tastes and budget. Crab, lobster, sea bass, monkfish and gurnard are all great options as well as the ever-popular cod.

## INGREDIENTS

4 tbsp vegetable oil or clarified butter

1 large onion, diced

2-4 cloves of garlic, sliced or crushed

1 tbsp mustard seeds

A good handful of curry leaves (about 30)

1 400g tin of chopped tomatoes

1 fresh tamarind pod

1-2 fresh chillies

2 tbsp ground coriander

2 tbsp turmeric

Your choice of seafood – about 6 prawns per person, or 200g fish fillets

## METHOD

First, prepare the ingredients. Tamarind pods are odd looking things, similar to a large monkey nut. Peel the outer casing off and remove the sticky nut inside. Soak this in 100ml of warm water and agitate with a fork. Once it's melted, pass the water through a sieve and set aside. Slice the chilli lengthways from the tip, stopping just short of the stem. This way, if you think the curry is getting a little too hot while you're cooking, you can easily pull the offending chilli out whole. It can always be put back if you change your mind.

Heat the oil in a saucepan and briefly fry the mustard seeds. Add the diced onion and let it sweat without browning. Add all the remaining ingredients except the seafood, and leave the curry base to gently simmer away. Make sure to check the sauce as it cooks to ensure the chilli isn't going to cause you a problem, and add salt to taste. It really is that simple.

To finish your curry, the choice of seafood is totally up to you, but the key is to not overcook it. If you are using prawns give them 5 minutes simmering in the sauce. Crab meat is already cooked so that will only need warming up. You can cook chunks of fish in the sauce too, depending on the size these should only need a few minutes. A real showstopper would be to roast a whole sea bass in a salt crust and serve it with the curry as an accompaniment. You could add some veg to the curry too; potatoes, cauliflower or okra would be great.

Preparation time: 5 minutes | Cooking time: approx. 5 minutes | Serves: as many as you like

# Sankey's

# BBQ TABASCO OYSTERS

We love oysters and are always trying new things. On a trip at the end of the summer to our friends Holly and Nick's house, we brought a box over, fully intending to just shuck them and eat them raw. But after a beer or two, Nick started his chiminea up to keep the girls warm and I couldn't help myself… I raided the kitchen for a few bits and hey presto, the BBQ Tabasco Oysters were born.

## INGREDIENTS

Salted butter

Banana shallots

Tabasco sauce (try the smoked chipotle one – it's incredible for this)

Oysters

## METHOD

Before you cook the oysters you need to make the sauce. Melt a knob of butter in a small saucepan. How much depends on how much sauce you want.

Dice a shallot and fry gently in the butter but don't let it brown. Then add a good few shakes of Tabasco sauce. It's important to do this right at the end or you will burn the kick out of it.

Ok, it's time for the oysters. Take each oyster and place into the glowing charcoal as they are, but make sure you get them the right way up. The top is slightly flatter than the bottom. After about 5 minutes the oysters will be cooked and the shells will have opened or become ajar. Careful, these are going to be very hot, so remove them from the coals using tongs.

Place the oysters, still in their shells, into a bowl balanced on foil so they stay the right way up. When they have cooled down enough to pick up, place in the palm of your hand and open the oyster with a blunt knife. Use a tea towel here to protect you from the hot liquid inside. Once they are all open, add a teaspoon of Tabasco butter to each one and you're good to go.

Preparation time: 10 minutes | Cooking time: 35 minutes | Serves: 2

# SANKEY'S

# EASY-PEASY SEAFOOD PAELLA

That delicious aroma, the amazing textures, incredible flavours of saffron, paprika and fresh seafood…it's unbeatable. We think we've totally nailed our paella and we've come up with a great hack for you to try at home. To nail this you are going to need to be extra prepared and get all the ingredients laid out ready to go. You can use a paella dish, or a large saucepan.

## INGREDIENTS

1 pinch of saffron

175-185g Arborio rice

2 tbsp olive oil

80g chorizo

2 chicken thighs
(skin off, bone out)

2 onions

2 peppers
(your choice of colour)

2 cloves of garlic, diced and mixed with olive oil

2 tbsp smoked paprika

284ml (½ pint) fish or chicken stock

Generous splash of white wine

10-12 cleaned mussels

1 squid tube cut into rings, fresh or frozen

½ pint glass of Greenland prawns, shell on

½ pint glass of Greenland prawns, shell off or king prawns, shell off

Small handful of chopped parsley

1 lemon, quartered

## METHOD

Our top tip is to par cook the rice in advance; this ensures that all your rice is cooked and that you won't over cook the fish. To do this, cook the rice with the saffron as per the instructions on the packet, but stop halfway through and drain.

Add the olive oil to the paella pan and then the chorizo and raw chicken. Once they are cooked through, add the onions and peppers to sweat down. Once the onions and peppers are cooked, make a small well in the centre, add the garlic and smoked paprika and fry off a little before mixing with the rest of the contents of the pan. Add the stock and the white wine and stir well.

When the stock has started to boil, add the squid, mussels and raw king prawns if using, placing the lid on top to trap the steam. Once the mussels have started to open, pour in the rice and gently mix into the stock, paying careful attention to the bottom of the pan to ensure it doesn't burn or stick. Add the shell on Greenland prawns and shell off Greenland prawns if using. Cook till the stock has been absorbed.

### To serve

Season to taste and serve with the parsley scattered on top and a wedge of lemon each. You can serve the paella in the pan or a serving dish, just make sure it's warm.

# GARDEN OF HEALTHY DELIGHTS

Blogger, photographer, mum, and advocate for healthy homemade meals as well as tasty treats… Severien Vits provides inspiration straight from the Garden of England to put good food on your family's table.

More Than Just Carrots is the name of Severien's blog, which is an online haven for healthy yet fun and appealing recipes for both parents and kids to make at home. Each post is accompanied by her own photography, which she got into through her food writing and developing dishes. There are articles and stories too on the subject of 'learning to eat' – Severien's thoughts and strategies about how and why to teach children the art of eating healthily and happily – which is a big part of her ethos when it comes to mealtimes.

"More Than Just Carrots is a product of my intentions as a mum, as well as my own love for fresh produce," says Severien. She moved to Kent with her husband and first child from London and enjoyed having the space and means to grow vegetables right from the start. Getting her kids involved means they are excited to eat the fruits of their labour, and aren't afraid to try new things. They can progress from the garden straight into the kitchen with Severien's recipes, especially created for kids and simply laid out on the blog with plenty of pictures to make following the steps easy and fun.

Severien's photography journey started because of her blogging, and she has learnt about photography through food and vice versa along the way. When she decided to try working for others as well, Severien visited Shipbourne Farmer's Market every week to photograph the people and produce. "It's a lovely, small weekly market with amazing produce and lovely people. It has a real sense of community, and brings together people who want to support local produce," says Severien.

Being self-taught, opportunities like this are valuable and have turned her hobby into a job, which in turn led to Tree of Hope approaching Severien to work on their Dine and Donate campaign, and then this book. She likes being involved in the community and discovering more ways to combine nutrition and flavour through food photography. Her own creations mingle traditional dishes from her home country of Belgium with Kent's wonderful produce, meeting the challenge of fun and varied healthy eating with an enduring love of food for the whole family.

Preparation time: 10 minutes | Cooking time: 30 minutes | Makes 600g (about 20 portions)

# Severien Vits

## CRISPY GRANOLA WITH PUFFED QUINOA AND CHOCOLATE CHIPS

This healthy crispy granola with puffed quinoa and chocolate chips is a great alternative to shop bought cereals. It's really crispy, has some sweetness but not too much, and there's even chocolate in it! The kids love it too and why wouldn't they? Just add fruit and yoghurt in the morning and breakfast will be ready in no time.

### INGREDIENTS

300g jumbo oats
150g sunflower seeds
75g pumpkin seeds
60g golden linseeds
75g puffed quinoa
3 tbsp coconut oil
(or rapeseed oil)
3 tbsp maple syrup (or honey)
50g chocolate chips

### METHOD

Preheat the oven to 180°c and gently mix together all the dry ingredients (not the chocolate chips). Combine the coconut oil with the maple syrup or honey and warm up briefly in the microwave to melt the coconut oil and to make the mixture very runny. Pour this mixture onto the dry ingredients and stir in gently. Try to coat all the oats and seeds without breaking up the oats too much.

Spread the mixture out in two baking trays with high enough sides to stir the granola during baking. Place the trays in the preheated oven for 10 minutes, then take them out and stir the granola well so it bakes on all sides. Repeat this twice more until golden and crispy.

Allow to cool down before adding the chocolate chips. Serve with fruit, yoghurt or toppings of your choice for a delicious and nutritious start to the day.

# By name and by nature

The clue to The Small Holding's ethos is in its name; the farm and kitchen showcases the best of the beautiful Kent countryside and the home-grown ingredients that it produces.

---

Brothers Will and Matt Devlin were already well-known in the Garden of England for their innovative pop-ups under the name No Fixed Abode. After a year of experimenting, refining, and playing around with exciting food and flavours which itself followed a ten-year career as chefs, they decided that a fixed abode was in fact just the thing they wanted next. A venue came up amidst its own acre of land, and by spring 2017 the boys were refurbishing and planting to their heart's content. The Small Holding – by name and by nature – encompasses everything that is important to them about eating and drinking: growing, freshness, flavour, and innovative cooking.

The kitchen team – Will and his other chef Harry – create the singular set menu from what's around them, which comes down to the season and even the day. Their dishes are inspired by walks through the farm past polytunnels, chickens, ducks and pigs as well as foraging in the nearby woodland. "We don't have to cook inside a box, so to speak," says Will, "as what we have here is unique, and we believe that growing ingredients ourselves results in the best flavour." The food is served by the chefs, connecting the whole experience from farm to fork, and complemented by Matt's knowledge of craft beer and perfect pairings from resident 'wine geek' Sally, who presides over a hand-picked collection from independent growers, including Kent's very own flourishing vineyards.

The compact team are committed to making a visit to The Small Holding a real experience. From the 20-seat dining area, there's a view of both the open kitchen and the farm, allowing guests to get in touch with the origins of their meal, and to witness the love and care that goes into producing it. An air of quality combined with a relaxed and cosy farmhouse kitchen-style restaurant and bar beautifully reflects what Will and Matt's venture is all about. If not grown on the farm itself, produce is currently sourced from someone the Devlin brothers know and is mostly very local, but they are still keen to continue expanding – putting The Small Holding's very own dairy and charcuterie on the menu, for example – and to stock up their proverbial and literal larder for many meals to come.

# The Small Holding

# ROAST DUCK WITH GOOSEBERRY AND COURGETTE

To create this recipe, we dry-aged our Indian runner ducks for 10 days to extract the most flavour out of them, and then simply roasted and paired them with other produce we had around us on the farm. The gooseberries cut nicely through the fat and everything balances really well.

## INGREDIENTS

**For the duck:**

1 whole free range duck

½ bunch of fresh thyme

½ bunch of fresh rosemary

100g good quality unsalted butter

50g sea salt flakes

**For the confit duck leg:**

100g flaked sea salt

1 litre duck fat

8 black peppercorns

8 juniper berries

1 star anise

1 cinnamon stick

**For the sauce:**

1 tbsp rapeseed oil

200g shallots, sliced

150ml Port

50ml Madeira

1 litre veal stock

**For the gooseberry ketchup:**

250g gooseberries

100g chardonnay vinegar

100g caster sugar

**To serve:**

10 leaves of mixed rainbow chard

2 young yellow courgettes

2 young green courgettes

## METHOD

Start by preparing your duck. Remove the legs, cover them with the 100g of salt and set aside for 1 hour. Remove the wishbone from the bird and then carefully remove the breasts, making sure you work with the knife close to the bone to remove all of the meat. Then remove the inner fillet and reserve for the sauce.

### For the confit duck leg

Wash off the salt and dry the duck legs. Put into a deep ovenproof roasting tray and cover with duck fat. Add all spices, cover with a sheet of greaseproof paper and two layers of tinfoil wrapped tightly over the top. Cook the duck at 100°c for 12 hours (overnight is best). Once the duck is cooked, set aside to cool in the fat until cool enough to touch. Lift the legs out and separate the meat from the bone and skin, making sure you remove all cartilage as well. Flake the meat into a pan with a few tablespoons of the cooking fat, ready to reheat before plating.

### For the sauce

Roughly dice the inner fillets and roast over a high heat in a heavy-based pan with the rapeseed oil. Once roasted, add the sliced shallots and cook until soft and translucent with no colour. Deglaze the pan with Port and Madeira and cook until the alcohol has burnt off. Then add the veal stock and reduce to a consistency that you are happy with.

### For the gooseberry ketchup

Add all ingredients to a pan, bring to the boil and then blitz in a blender until smooth.

### To serve

Wash the chard and slice the courgettes; it doesn't matter what shape as long as they are all even sizes. To roast the duck, season the breast with Maldon salt. Place skin side down in a cold ovenproof pan, turn the heat on low and allow the fat to render down. Once the skin is golden brown put the frying pan in the oven at 180°c for 7 minutes if you like your duck pink, a little longer if you don't. Take the duck out of the pan and leave it to rest skin side up so all the fat can baste the meat. Discard half of the duck fat from the frying pan (save for your Sunday roast potatoes!) and add the courgettes. Roast until they have a nice golden colour, then turn the heat down and add the chard to wilt it. Warm the confit duck leg through and then place a spoonful of the meat onto the serving plate. Add some chard, roasted courgettes and a slice of duck breast. Finish with a drizzle of sauce and a little gooseberry ketchup.

# Naturally good for you

Husband and wife team Ben and Kirsty Sulston have set up a restaurant based on their love of healthy, tasty food full of natural flavour and local produce.

Sulston's Kitchen started life as a YouTube channel featuring healthy recipes from Ben and Kirsty, the couple who began the venture based on a passion for food that tastes good and does you good. Their videos and initial events got plenty of enthusiastic feedback, so Ben and Kirsty knew there was demand for their kind of cooking. Meanwhile, they were both still working full-time and drawing on ideas from Kirsty's career as a personal trainer and nutritionist, and Ben's background as a chef for over 20 years. He went out to Phuket to consult on the setting up of a new restaurant for a friend, and knew then that he and Kirsty could do the same back home.

The concept behind the food at Sulston's Kitchen is to bring out the best in great ingredients by using natural flavours that already have health benefits. Breakfasts, lunches, smoothies, snacks and refreshing drinks are all made from scratch in the restaurant, with careful consideration of what goes into each dish. Little changes such as only using coconut oil and extra-virgin olive oil, swapping refined sugars for fruit, honey or maple syrup and seasoning with Cornish sea salt that's full of minerals make a big difference to both taste and the benefits for your body.

Eating and drinking well plays an integral part in maintaining a balanced lifestyle for the driven couple, who now have a one year old son, Sebastian, already a regular customer! The friendly, family feel at Sulston's is something Ben and Kirsty have cultivated with a relaxed, rustic space for daytimes during the week, which doubles as an evening venue for their monthly supper clubs. These have proved a great place to meet new people, which Ben and Kirsty really encourage.

"We're working towards even more of a community here," says Ben, "and that applies to our suppliers as well; we've got a fishmongers in the next village, the butcher on our street, freshly roasted coffee from Canterbury, and all our fruit comes from orchards around Kent." As a team of just two, running a business to such high standards and ethics is demanding but Ben and Kirsty love and believe in what they do. Plans for the future involve continuing to enjoy the ride as their venture develops, with health, happiness, and super tasty food always at its core!

Preparation time: 20 minutes | Cooking time: 2 hours | Serves: 4

# SULSTON'S KITCHEN

# HARISSA SPICED CHICKEN WITH A WARM FREEKEH, SWEET POTATO, FETA AND POMEGRANATE SALAD

This dish has an important place in our hearts, as it's a take on our signature dish and was the first dish we ever sold at Sulston's Kitchen. It still makes a regular appearance on the specials board and at our Supper Clubs.

## INGREDIENTS

**For the harissa spiced chicken:**
1 medium chicken
10g dry harissa spice mix
1 lemon, cut in half
1 bulb of garlic, cut in half
2 sprigs of rosemary
2 sprigs of thyme
30g honey

**For the salad:**
100g feta
175g baby spinach
5 sprigs of coriander
1 pomegranate
300g sweet potato
30g pumpkin seeds
Drizzle of coconut oil
150g freekeh
450ml white chicken stock

**To serve:**
1 lemon, juiced
25ml extra-virgin olive oil

## METHOD

**For the harissa spiced chicken**

Coat the chicken with the harissa spice mix and stuff the cavity with the lemon, garlic, rosemary and thyme. Place onto a baking dish and put into a preheated oven at 200°c for 45 minutes. Baste the chicken throughout the cooking process by spooning the cooking liquor over the chicken. Try to do this every 20 minutes. Remove from the oven and drizzle with honey. Place back in the oven for a further 10 minutes then drop the temperature to 180°c and cook for a further 45 minutes, remembering to baste. Remove from the oven and allow to rest for 25 minutes before carving. When carved, pour all of the cooking juices into a jug to serve.

**For the salad**

This can be done while the chicken is resting, but the salad can be served hot or cold so you can make it up in the morning or even the day before so you can spend more time with your guests. Take it out of the fridge 1 hour before you are going to eat.

Dice the feta into 2cm cubes. Wash and roughly chop the spinach and coriander. Gently roll the pomegranate then cut in half and squeeze over a bowl, tapping the outside with a spoon if the seeds don't fall out easily. Keep all the juice and seeds.

Peel and chop the sweet potato into 3cm cubes, place onto a baking tray with the pumpkin seeds, drizzle with a little coconut oil and then cook at 200°c for 20 minutes.

Cover the freekeh with the chicken stock and bring to the boil. Turn down to a simmer and cook until all the liquid has evaporated. Remove from the stove, place a lid on top and allow to sit for 10 minutes.

**To serve**

Mix the feta, spinach, coriander, pomegranate juice and seeds, sweet potato, pumpkin seeds, lemon juice and olive oil into the cooked freekeh and then transfer everything to a serving dish. Refrigerate if making in advance, or serve straight away while still warm with the carved spiced chicken.

**Chef's tip**

Keep the chicken carcass and use it to make a bone broth or soup.

Preparation time: 10 minutes, plus freezing time | Serves: 2

# SULSTON'S KITCHEN

# KENTISH STRAWBERRIES, WATERMELON, CHIA AND COCONUT SMOOTHIE

When strawberries are in season in the UK, their taste is hard to beat. They are one of our favourite fruits, and we're lucky enough to be able to get delightful Kentish strawberries from our local veg supplier. This year we created this delicious and nutritious smoothie.

## INGREDIENTS

200g watermelon
300g strawberries
20g chia seeds
200g coconut milk
100g coconut water
200g bananas

## METHOD

### The day before

Peel the watermelon and roughly dice, place onto a tray and freeze. You can dice a whole watermelon and then store the cubes in containers when frozen for future smoothies. Hull the strawberries, cut them into quarters, place onto a tray and freeze.

### To make the smoothie

Put everything into the blender. Start on a low speed, then increase slowly to a medium-high speed and blend until smooth. Pour into glasses and enjoy.

### Chef's tip

Using coconut water and milk rather than just water not only adds flavour but extra nutrients too, and by freezing the fruit you don't need to add ice as this dilutes the flavour and has no nutritional value.

# Eclectic and Quirky

Vittle and Swig takes a contemporary approach to British cuisine, serving unusual cocktails in a relaxed atmosphere.

The owners of Vittle and Swig, Gerry Stevens and Alex Blaber, have combined drinking and dining to create their casual bar and restaurant in the busy town of Tunbridge Wells. They wanted to create a place where guests could enjoy a draft beer, great wine or a cocktail with a twist as well as a delicious lunch or evening meal. The couple met in 2014 when the restaurant was Camden Quarter; in 2016 they had the opportunity to buy the restaurant and took it over to form Vittle and Swig. They welcomed back all the old staff – including their valued sous chef, Nathan Coleman – and their regular customers, but updated the feel and look of the restaurant to realise their own vision for it.

Alex, the head chef, describes the food as modern British, in the sense that it reflects the multiculturalism of today's cuisine, with influences and flavours coming from all over the world. He loves having such a variety of ingredients to work with, and says how lucky they are being close enough to benefit from London's markets, yet surrounded by Kentish countryside which offers a fantastic range of local produce and a great place for foraging their own seasonal wild ingredients. The restaurant uses a fish supplier based in Sevenoaks, who have their own boats so the catch is always really fresh, and a specialist supplier based in Tonbridge who can source top quality ingredients from anywhere. This approach means the kitchen team can work with the best raw materials to create their eclectic yet elegant dishes.

It's not just the food and drink drawing crowds at Vittle and Swig though; since Gerry and Alex took on the venture they have introduced regular events to the restaurant's calendar, which are held in the spacious upstairs room and adjacent cocktail bar that also plays host to private parties and occasions when hired out. The comedy nights in particular have been really popular, so the pair plan to put on cabaret nights as well, and will soon launch their Swig Society, inviting members to sample different drinks paired with some interesting food combinations. Summer 2018 saw them launch their first six course tasting menu matched with drink courses. Its success has promoted plans to introduce four tasting menus a year, incorporating the changing ingredients of the seasons.

VITTLE
and
SWIG

RESTAURANT · BAR · CAFE

Preparation time: 1 hour 45 minutes, plus 4-6 hours for the labneh | Cooking time: 2 hours
Serves: 4 as a starter or 2 as a light lunch

# VITTLE AND SWIG

# SPICED COD CHEEKS AND SALT BAKED BEETROOT

A few chef's tips: pierce a hole in the wrapped beetroots before baking as they have been known to explode in the oven. Scallops and hazelnuts are great alternatives to cod cheeks and cobnuts.

## INGREDIENTS

**For the labneh:**

1 tsp each of coriander, caraway and cumin seeds

½ tsp sumac

250g Greek yoghurt

1 tbsp olive oil

1 lemon, juiced and zested

1 tsp chopped thyme leaves

1 clove of garlic, finely grated

**For the salt baked beetroot:**

1kg mixed medium-sized heritage beetroots (ruby, candy and golden)

300g each of table salt and plain flour

135g egg white

**For the carrot dressing:**

500g large carrots

120ml olive oil

1 tsp each of chopped thyme and tarragon

Pinch of salt and sugar

50ml white wine vinegar

100ml each of Madeira (or other sweet wine) and orange juice

**For the cobnuts:**

500g Kentish cobnuts, shelled

50g butter, melted

**To serve:**

12 fresh cod cheeks

Large pinch of Cajun spice and salt

3 tbsp vegetable oil

Pinch of fennel pollen

Frisée leaves, to garnish

## METHOD

**For the labneh**

Toast the seeds in a dry pan until fragrant and lightly smoky, then grind to a powder and mix with the sumac. Combine the yoghurt, olive oil, half the lemon zest and juice, thyme, garlic and half the spices. Taste, adding more spice if preferred. Line a sieve over a bowl with muslin, transfer the yoghurt mixture into the sieve, tie the cloth with string and hang in the fridge for 4 to 6 hours.

**For the salt baked beetroot**

Preheat the oven to 180°c. Beat the salt, flour and egg white in a stand mixer on a medium speed for 2 minutes. Slowly add 120ml of water until a slightly sticky dough comes together. Cover and rest in the fridge for 5 minutes. Wash and dry the beetroots. Portion the dough to flatted pieces about 1cm thick and double the circumference of the beetroot. Encase each beetroot in dough then cook on a baking tray in the preheated oven for around 1 hour. Check they are soft with a skewer then leave to cool. Crack them open, scrape the skin away and cut into a variety of shapes.

**For the carrot dressing**

Peel and finely dice 75g of the carrots. Blend trimmings and the remaining carrots to get 150ml of juice. Place half the olive oil in a saucepan on a medium heat, add the diced carrots, and sweat gently for a few minutes before adding the thyme, tarragon, salt and sugar. Add vinegar, reduce until nearly dry, then add the Madeira and reduce by half. Add the carrot and orange juice and reduce by half again, then add the rest of the olive oil and simmer for 2 minutes.

**For the cobnuts**

Coat the nuts in butter and season with a pinch of salt, roast at 160°c for 30 to 40 minutes or until golden and crunchy.

**To serve**

Dress the beetroot with a little olive oil and arrange along one side of the plate. Spoon blobs of labneh onto the beetroots, drizzle over some carrot dressing, then scatter crushed cobnuts on top.

Carefully peel the outer membrane on one side of each cod cheek. Dry the cheeks on kitchen towel and season generously with Cajun spice and salt. Heat the oil in a non-stick frying pan until lightly smoking and then cook the cheeks for 1 to 2 minutes until golden. Turn over, remove from the heat, add a knob of butter and the remaining lemon juice to the pan then rest for 1 to 2 minutes. Drain and place next to the beetroot. Spoon a little dressing onto the cheeks, sprinkle over the fennel pollen and finish with the frisée leaves. Serve immediately.

# IT'S AN ESTATE OF MIND

Fresh, seasonal food sourced from The Warren's own estate is the centrepiece at the stylish, quirky restaurant in Tunbridge Wells.

Chris Fitt and Martin Haynes set up The Warren in March 2016, having taken over the premises in an iconic location on Tunbridge Wells' High Street. They completely refurbed the interior, adding their own touch – which has been described as quirky and eccentric – to the upstairs dining space. Once you've looked up, spotted the conservatory windows and ascended, you'll be welcomed into a warm and cosy restaurant where eclectic artwork, chandeliers glittering overhead and a baby grand piano complete with live pianist on Fridays and Saturdays set the mood.

This unique reception is completed by the front of house team, headed up by maître d' Magdalena, the star of the show. Their diverse backgrounds bring a host of skills and professional European hospitality to the table, including head barman Olivier's extensive knowledge of wine and interesting cocktails. Of spirits and beers, the golden rule is three outstanding options for each tipple, sticking to the 'quality over quantity' motto that the restaurant team like to work to. They also try to source from local producers as much as possible, and it doesn't get much closer to home than their own Crowborough Warren Estate.

The restaurateurs owned land and raised livestock including poultry, wild boar, Sussex cattle, sheep, fallow deer, poultry and pigs before The Warren came into existence, but it seemed like a perfect way to cut out the middle man. As a result, the menu at the restaurant is full of both modern and traditional British dishes made with lamb, hogget, mutton, beef, pork, boar, venison and more which is butchered on the estate and finished in the kitchen at The Warren. The chefs, helmed by head chef Robert Marshall, are given plenty of license to create interesting food with ingredients from the nose to the tail of the animal, plus foraged delicacies like sea purslane and hand-dived crayfish.

The team are always on the lookout for new and delicious produce to put on the menu, and have just put up their first polytunnels on the estate as part of the journey towards self-sufficiency. The restaurant offers something different both from an aesthetic and a foodie perspective, so has gained a reputation as Tunbridge Wells' destination spot for occasions. Part of the ethos at The Warren is about making great food, beautifully prepared, accessible to everyone so whether you fancy a drink or a three course meal, class and quirkiness awaits.

Preparation time: 1 hour plus 1 day | Cooking time: 1 hour | Serves: 6

# THE WARREN

## SADDLE OF VENISON

With our estate supplying so many of our ingredients, our food is naturally very seasonal. We serve this rich and earthy dish during the autumn, with the onset of game season. Using prime cuts with those less glamorous, or the trimmings as we have here, is a great way of using the whole animal.

## INGREDIENTS

### For the loin:
120-150g trimmed venison loin per person (a whole saddle will feed as many as 20 people)
Vegetable or pomace oil (you could use dripping as we do)

### For the sauce:
All the venison bones
Carrots, celery, and onions, roughly chopped
Few cloves of garlic, crushed
Sprinkling of mustard powder
300ml Port
100ml red wine
20g malt extract
A few bay leaves, star anise and cloves
A dash of red wine vinegar, to taste

### For the bramble compote:
100g white sugar
100ml each red wine vinegar and blackberry liqueur
A handful or so of blackberries, washed gently in cold water

### For the pie:
All the venison trimmings, diced
Same quantity of carrots, celery and onion as the meat, neatly diced
2 cloves of garlic, crushed
700ml red wine
A couple of bay leaves and thyme sprigs
1 tbsp tomato purée
Sprinkling of dark brown sugar
1 pack of ready-rolled puff pastry
1 whole egg and 1 yolk
Handful of hogweed seeds, soaked overnight then dried in a warm place

## METHOD

### Method
First, remove the loin from the saddle. Trim the loins and discard any sinew but keep the meat. Remove as much of the meat from the bones as you can, add to the trim from the loins, dice this all up and set aside.

### For the sauce
Start this a day or so beforehand. Roast the bones in an oven at 200°c for 1 to 2 hours or until they have good colour. Transfer the bones to a large stock pot already at a simmer, thoroughly deglaze the roasting tray and then add the juices to the stock. Simmer without boiling for at least 24 hours then skim, strain and reserve.

Colour the veg in a heavy-based pan. Stir in the mustard powder, cook out for 1 minute then add the Port and wine. Reduce until syrupy, add the bulk of the stock (reserving some for the pies), the malt extract and aromatics then reduce to a sauce consistency. Strain, adjust the seasoning, add a dash of the vinegar and set aside.

### For the bramble compote
Bring the sugar and vinegar to the boil, add the bramble liqueur and flambé to burn off the alcohol. Remove from the heat, chill, add the brambles, and allow to steep.

### For the pie
Colour the venison trimmings in a pan with a little oil. Add the diced vegetables and cook until just soft. Add the wine, and reduce until almost gone. Add the herbs, a touch of tomato purée (to help thicken and enrich the pie filling) and the remaining stock. Stew until the meat is tender. Add brown sugar to taste; this is to soften the tannins of the wine, but the pie should not be sweet.

Lightly score the pastry, glaze it with egg and sprinkle over hogweed seeds. Bake at 200°c for 8 to10 minutes.

### For the loin
Season well with salt. Colour in a hot pan, turning every 30 seconds or so. Move the meat to a roasting tray, season again, and roast at 200°c for 10 to 15 minutes until the centre of the loin reaches approximately 45°c. Rest the meat in a warm place for 5 to 10 minutes. Resting is essential; carve too soon and the meat won't be as moist.

### To serve
Arrange the prepared accompaniments on warmed plates with a few slices of loin, ready the pie(s), and dress, artfully, with the blackberry sauce and any seasonal herbs you choose, even better if gathered from nearby.

Add sauce to your liking, or serve on the side if preferred.

# The Great British Pub

The Chaser Inn is where it all began for Whiting & Hammond, an award-winning company with a brood of eight family-run pubs across Kent, Surrey and Sussex, which now includes The Little Brown Jug in Chiddingstone Causeway and The King's Head in Bessels Green.

The summer of 2003 saw the grand opening of Whiting & Hammond's flagship pub, The Chaser Inn, which is surrounded by an expanse of grassy common with spectacular views, the beautiful church of St Giles and the village of Shipbourne. The building underwent extensive refurbishment to create the comfortable, friendly environment for dining and drinking that it is today. The Chaser Inn takes its name from an illustrious history involving the Queen Mother's steeplechase horses, which were trained on the nearby Fairlawn Estate by Major Peter Cazalet, who built the pub as a family home in 1880. Connecting past with present, the Chaser's guests can now enjoy a locally renowned Sunday lunch in the stunning Church Room, Jockey Room, or unique all-weather courtyard. Time-honoured traditions are a huge part of what makes The Chaser Inn special, along with the emphasis on individuality and valued staff within each branch of the Whiting & Hammond family.

This ethos extends to all the pubs under the company umbrella, including the third venture which started small but aimed big and is now the location of Whiting & Hammond's head office. The Little Brown Jug is home to one-of-a-kind dining experiences in the garden, legendary beer festivals, and a real community atmosphere thanks to all the locals who have made it their regular pit-stop for pints and a plate of beer-battered fish and chips (comes in small or whale-sized portions). This customer favourite is shared by punters at The King's Head, a recent addition to the group in the leafy suburb of Sevenoaks. A country pub with all the trimmings and then some – like the heated tiki huts – it's ideal and within easy reach for those in the inner circle who enjoy an honest meal and good cask ale.

It's important to the team at every Whiting & Hammond pub that their classic dishes are freshly prepared, sourced locally and part of a daily changing menu. Using British ingredients is championed by the managers, who say it's better for the environment, an important boost for the local economy, and a matter of pride with the staff. The community spirit and focus on great food and drink in every new venture has been maintained by Brian Whiting, originally a chef by trade, who joined forces with Chris Hammond to begin the company's journey. Their drive and ambition started it all, and continues to bring proper pubs to Kent and beyond, where people can be assured of a warm welcome, an inviting atmosphere, and of course, some fantastic food and drink.

Preparation time: 15 minutes | Cooking time: 15 minutes | Serves: 4

# The King's Head

# SAUTÉED ASPARAGUS SPEARS, POACHED FREE RANGE EGG, GLAZED HOLLANDAISE, SHAVED WILTSHIRE TRUFFLE

There may only be a handful of ingredients but using the freshest, locally-sourced Kent asparagus makes this dish spectacular. Ready in a matter of minutes, it's a perfect starter or light lunch option.

## INGREDIENTS

**For the hollandaise:**
4 egg yolks
250g clarified butter, warmed
1 tbsp white wine vinegar
Lemon juice, to taste

**For the asparagus:**
20 Kentish asparagus spears
1 Wiltshire truffle, shaved (optional)

**For the poached egg:**
4 free-range eggs
2 litres water
80ml white wine vinegar

## METHOD

**For the hollandaise**

Place the egg yolks and white wine vinegar in a bowl over a pan of simmering water, and whisk constantly until the volume has doubled in size and can hold a ribbon shape. Remove the bowl from the water then very slowly whisk in the clarified butter until a nice thick sauce has formed. Season the hollandaise and whisk in a squeeze of lemon juice according to personal taste. Use as soon as possible.

**For the asparagus**

Snap each asparagus spear near the bottom to break off the woody part and discard it. Peel downwards from just below the tip. Place in a pan of boiling salted water and boil for 2 minutes or until tender, then drain the water away.

**For the poached egg**

Bring the water and vinegar to the boil in a large saucepan, give it a gentle whisk and then crack the eggs into the water. Bring back to the boil then reduce to a simmering boil for 3 minutes. Remove each egg very carefully with a slotted spoon.

**To serve**

Place five asparagus spears on each plate, cover the peeled part of the asparagus with 3 tablespoons of hollandaise and then place the plates under a preheated grill until the sauce is golden. Remove from the grill, add a freshly poached egg to each plate and sprinkle the freshly shaved Wiltshire truffle all over.

Preparation time: 25 minutes | Cooking time: 45-50 minutes | Serves 12

# The Chaser Inn

# BAKED NEW YORK-STYLE CHEESECAKE WITH CLEMENTINE COMPOTE

This baked cheesecake has been a firm favourite every time it's appeared on The Chaser's menu. A gentle hand while mixing together will ensure a light and beautifully set cheesecake. We like to add strawberries and drizzle some of the clementine sauce on the plate as well.

## INGREDIENTS

**For the cheesecake:**
135g plain digestive biscuits
60g unsalted butter, melted
845g full-fat soft cheese
200g caster sugar
60g cornflour
2 vanilla pods
5 free-range eggs
375ml double cream

**For the clementine compote:**
4 clementines, juiced
3 tbsp caster sugar
8 clementines, peeled and segmented

## METHOD

**For the cheesecake**

Start by lining a 25cm wide and 5cm deep spring-form cake tin with baking paper and place it on a baking tray. Blitz the digestives in a blender or food processor until you have fine crumbs, then add the melted butter and blitz until mixed through. Press evenly into the base of the tin, ensuring that it's completely smooth, and place in the fridge for 30 minutes.

Preheat the oven to 145°c. In a mixer, beat the soft cheese, caster sugar, cornflour and seeds from the vanilla pods on a medium speed, adding one egg at a time to make sure that it's fully incorporated. Once the eggs are added, add the cream and stir until incorporated, but be careful not to over-mix, as this will cause cracks in the cheesecake once cooked. Pour over the biscuit base, and gently shake the tin to level the filling. Place in the middle of the oven to cook for approximately 45 minutes until set (it should have a slight wobble in the centre, with a nice golden top), then allow to cool.

**For the clementine compote**

While the cheesecake is cooling, place the clementine juice and caster sugar in a saucepan on a gentle heat, until the sugar dissolves and the juice starts to thicken. Add the clementine segments and remove from the heat. Allow to cool, then spoon over the top of the cheesecake for decoration.

Preparation time: 45 minutes | Cooking time: 1 hour | Serves 4

# THE LITTLE BROWN JUG

# ROASTED FILLET OF COD WITH JERUSALEM ARTICHOKES, MUSSELS AND CHORIZO

You'll always find a selection of fish dishes on our menus, and this autumnal dish beautifully combines elements from the sea, the land and the earth. The Jerusalem artichoke is nutty, sweet and crunchy, the perfect accompaniment to fresh fish.

## INGREDIENTS

**For the roast artichokes:**

400g Jerusalem artichokes, washed and peeled

10g butter

25ml vegetable oil

2 cloves of garlic

1 sprig of thyme

1 tsp lemon juice

10g dill, chopped

**For the artichoke purée:**

200g Jerusalem artichokes, washed, peeled and diced

75ml vegetable stock

75ml semi-skimmed milk

**For the cod:**

2 tbsp vegetable oil

Salt and pepper

4 cod fillets

**For the mussels and chorizo:**

50g chorizo, diced small

1 clove of garlic, peeled and thinly sliced

1 small shallot, peeled and chopped

2 tbsp vegetable oil

500g mussels, cleaned

100ml dry white wine

100ml double cream

## METHOD

Preheat the oven to 180°c.

**For the roast artichokes**

Start by preparing the artichokes, halving the large ones and leaving the small ones whole. Place in a roasting tray and toss with the butter, oil, garlic and thyme. Roast in the preheated oven for approximately 40 to 50 minutes, until tender inside and crisp outside. To finish, toss the roasted artichokes with the lemon juice and chopped dill.

**For the artichoke purée**

While the artichokes are roasting, make the purée by adding all of the ingredients to a pan and bring to a gentle simmer to cook until the artichoke is soft. Blitz in a liquidiser until smooth.

**For the cod**

Once the purée is 5 minutes from being ready, start cooking the cod. Lightly coat a non-stick frying pan with the vegetable oil over a medium to high heat. When the pan is hot, season the cod fillets with salt and pepper and place skin-side down in the pan. Cook for 2 to 3 minutes until golden and crisp, then carefully turn over and cook the other side for another 2 to 3 minutes. Once the fish has turned opaque, it's ready to serve.

**For the mussels and chorizo**

Start the mussels when the cod fillets have just been turned over. In a separate pan, cook the chorizo, garlic and shallot in the oil on a medium heat until the shallot and garlic are cooked, then add the mussels and white wine. Cover with a lid and cook for approximately 2 to 3 minutes, until all of the mussels have opened (don't serve any mussels that haven't opened). Remove the mussels, reduce the cooking liquid by half and add the cream, then bring to the boil and serve as a sauce .

**To serve**

Place a spoonful of the artichoke purée on one side of the plate, place the back of the spoon into the middle of it and then drag to the other side of the plate. Gently lay the cod fillet on top of the purée skin side up. Top with a few mussels, pour over some chorizo sauce, and serve with the roasted artichokes. You could even top it off with some micro herbs for that restaurant-style finish.

# WAKE UP AND SMELL THE WHOLEFOODS

Debbie Stranack started Wholefood Wakeup in her own kitchen, creating nourishing food using ingredients such as raw veggies, plant proteins and healthy fats that do you good and taste amazing!

Wholefood Wakeup is, as the name suggests, about realising the benefits of eating well by finding wholesome alternatives to foods that don't do your body much good. It was created by Debbie Stranack as part of her own journey to better health and overcoming a constant and debilitating sleepiness. She started reading up on nutrition and applying what she learned to her other passion which has always been cooking, finally training to be a health coach in 2016. Finding alternatives to refined sugar was the first step, which is where irresistible desserts like her raw chocolates and marbled berry cashew cake came in. Debbie enjoyed cooking this way for herself and her husband, Gaston, so much that they both embraced the change wholeheartedly and now choose the food they eat for its nutrient qualities as much as its taste.

What surprised Debbie was the amount of restaurants lacking this kind of food on their menus. She wanted to encourage the introduction of nutritious plant-based dishes to the trade so that people aiming to balance healthy options with eating out have options. She started working with a fitness food company to build up their vegetarian offering, and plans to provide further consulting work in the industry for all kinds of food-led businesses.

A large part of Wholefood Wakeup is about sharing enjoyable ways to eat healthily, so Debbie also runs workshops at her home, individually or in groups of up to six, to teach people her tricks for incorporating more plant-based wholefoods into everyday eating. The workshops cover lots of healthy treats as well as savoury meals and are all entirely dairy- and gluten-free. Each workshop includes a homemade lunch that shows how tasty nutritious alternatives to shop bought and processed foods can be.

It's about more than just health for Debbie; in her own words, the most important thing when making changes to your eating habits is making whatever you choose to eat taste delicious. Sharing the journey towards feeling better with her husband Gaston has given them both a new and exciting direction when it comes to food, and for Debbie the creative and inventive aspects of her business continue to drive her forward.

Preparation time: 20 minutes, plus 30 minutes freezing then overnight to set | Serves: 10

# WHOLEFOOD WAKEUP

## MARBLED BERRY CASHEW CAKE

A creamy and nutritious plant-based dessert full of antioxidants, fibre, plant protein and healthy fats. So wholesome that you can eat it for breakfast! The cake here is made with foraged blackberries, but you can use blueberries, raspberries or even other colour-dense fruit like mango.

## INGREDIENTS

**For the base:**

100g cashew nuts
100g whole walnuts
100g soft Medjool dates, pitted
1 tbsp coconut oil
½ tsp ground cinnamon
½ tsp vanilla paste
Pinch of Himalayan salt

**For the filling:**

300g cashew nuts, soaked overnight and drained
1 400ml tin of coconut milk
6 tbsp maple syrup
2 tbsp melted coconut oil
1 tsp vanilla paste
175g berries (blackberries, blueberries, raspberries) or mango
Small pinch of Himalayan salt

## METHOD

**For the base**

Line an 18cm (or 20cm for a shallower cake) springform cake tin with non-stick liner. Place the cashew nuts whole into a food processor and process until finely ground. Add the remaining ingredients for the base and process until a dough just comes together, stopping regularly to check by squeezing the mixture between your fingers to see if the dough holds. Take care not to over-process the nuts as they will become too oily. Once you have dough, press it into your cake tin and place in the freezer for half an hour before adding the filling.

**For the filling**

Make sure all the ingredients are at room temperature for best results. Blend all the ingredients for the filling in a high speed blender. Pour the filling over the chilled base and return to the freezer until solid. If you want to marble the cake or set it into two layers, prepare the mixture without the fruit and then divide it into two 500ml amounts. Blend each with different colour fruits. To marble the cake, dollop the two colours alternately into the pan and use a skewer or chopstick to swirl the surface prettily. To create layers, freeze the first layer before adding the second. I like to keep a small amount of the bottom layer to swirl into the top.

**To serve**

Move the cake from the freezer to the fridge a few hours before serving so that you can slice it easily. Serve the cake plain, or decorate with fresh berries. Once served, I suggest slicing the leftover cake and returning these slices to the freezer, separated with greaseproof paper, so that you can remove them a slice at a time to defrost.

# THANK YOU

Back in May 2018 this book was just a dream but with an amazing team of passionate and incredibly talented volunteers and professionals behind us, we have created a book that captures the heart of the foodie scene running through Sevenoaks, Tonbridge, Tunbridge Wells and the beautiful villages that surround it. Thank you to each of you for believing in this project.

Thank you to Caroline Kings for your enthusiasm and passion for the book throughout. Your knowledge of food, restaurants and West Kent has enabled us to deliver a book that would connect with every reader and home cook.

Thank you to Severien Vits for tirelessly snapping every photo you see in this book. Your beautiful photos capture the true essence and character of every person, dish, restaurant and scenery that has had the privilege of crossing paths with you and your camera.

Thank you to Charlotte Rogers, an invaluable member of the team whose love of local eateries ensured we created a book that every food lover, avid restaurant goer and home cook will enjoy.

Thank you to Dan Smith, who captured the idea of this book and turned our rambling ideas into a front cover that is a contemporary work of art. One that we hope will stay on cook book shelves forever.

Thank you to Jess Htay your publishing knowledge and experience guided us through this whole project.

Thank you to Meze Publishing for your incredible support, good humour, and guidance throughout. The whole team have been a dream to work with.

Thank you to every single restaurant, chef and producer who has contributed to this book, for opening the doors of your kitchens, sharing your favourite recipes and enabling us to produce a cook book that so beautifully represents the food community and kitchens we are so proud to have in West Kent.

Thank you to each and every one of you, who has bought a copy of this book. We hope you love it, will treasure it forever and refer to it for cooking inspiration in years to come. The money raised from every copy sold will enable Tree of Hope to transform the lives of thousands of seriously ill and disabled children in the UK.

And finally thanks to the entire Tree of Hope team. Without their help, support and belief The Cook Book would not have been successfully published.

# Farmers' Markets

These fantastic farmers' markets are a great way to shop local and support our producers in West Kent.

---

## Tonbridge Farmers' Market

Sovereign Way
Tonbridge
TN9 1RG

*Held on the second Sunday of the month from 9:30am to 1:30pm.*
*There are usually more than 50 stalls, at this award winning market selling food, home and garden and craft items.*

## Tunbridge Wells (Town Hall) Farmers' Market

Crescent Road
Royal Tunbridge Wells
TN1 1RS

*Held every second and fourth Saturday of the month from 9:00am to 2:00pm.*
*Tunbridge Wells Farmers' Market was started by the Borough Council in September 1999. Now, there are around 40 stalls outside the Town Hall and products cover the whole range of local foods from goat's meat sausages to onion bhaji.*

## Tunbridge Wells (Pantiles) Food & Craft Market

The Pantiles
Royal Tunbridge Wells
TN2 5TN

*Held on the first and third full weekends of the month from 10:00am to 4:00pm.*
*This market revives the tradition of the open air market staged at the same venue several centuries ago.*

## Penshurst Farmers' Market

Penshurst Place Car Park
Penshurst Place
Penshurst
Nr Tonbridge
TN11 8DG

*Held on the first Saturday of every month from 9:30am to 12 noon.*
*In 2015 this market was named as the Best Farmers' Market by Kent Food and Drink Awards and was also listed by The Times in its top ten markets in the UK.*

## Hildenborough Farmers' Market

St. John's Church Centre
Tonbridge Road
Hildenborough
Nr Tonbridge
TN11 9HT

*Held every Tuesday from 9:00am to 11:00am.*
*Hildenborough Farmers' Market was started in 2008 and has grown steadily ever since. There is now an average of 20 stalls each week selling a variety of food, home and garden and craft items.*

## Sevenoaks Saturday Market

Blighs Meadow
off Pembroke Road
Sevenoaks
TN13 1DA

*Held every Saturday from 9:00am to 4:00pm.*
*A well-established market with many varieties of arts and crafts stalls. This market is being developed by the Town Council into a Farmers' Market with locally sourced food and drink.*

## West Malling Farmers' Market

High Street
West Malling
Kent

*Held on the fourth Sunday of every month from 9:30am to 1:30pm.*
*This market hosts a great array of farm produced meats, fruit, vegetables and cheeses, as well as artisan breads and cakes.*

## Shipbourne Farmers' Market

St Giles' Church
Stumble Hill
Shipbourne
TN11 9PF

*Held on the first Thursday of every month from 9:00am to 11:00am.*
*This award-winning market was listed in the Times and Telegraph as one of the Ten Best Farmers' Markets in the country. There is a loyalty card available for regular customers.*

## Knockholt 'Keep it Local' at Coolings

Coolings Gardener's Garden Centre
Rushmore Hill
Knockholt
Nr Sevenoaks
TN14 7NN

*Held on the fourth Saturday of every month from 9:00am to 1:00pm.*
*In October 2015, the market was awarded a "Highly Commended" certificate in the prestigious Kent Food & Drink Awards run by Kent Life magazine and Kent on Sunday newspaper. It was judged by the readers to be in the top three of the 50 or so markets across Kent.*

## Offham Farmers' Market

Spadework Nursery
Teston Road
West Malling
ME19 5NA

*Held on the second Saturday of each month from March to December, 10:00am to 1:00pm.*
*The market is organised by Spadework, a charity which provides training and support for adults with learning difficulties and other disabilities, and all pitch fees go directly to the charity. There's a great atmosphere at the market, and there are often live music and cookery demonstrations to enjoy.*

## Lamberhurst Village Market

Lamberhurst Memorial Hall
The Broadway
Lamberhurst
TN3 8DB

*Held on the first Wednesday of the month from 9:00am to 12 noon.*
*There are a variety of food, home and garden and craft stalls and the café donates its profits to the Hospice in the Weald.*

## Cranbrook Farmers' Market

Vestry Hall
High Street
Cranbrook
TN17 3HF

*Held every fourth Saturday from 9:30am to 1:00pm.*
*With an average of 14 stalls plus guest stallholders, the market offers one free stall per month to a charity or community stall.*

*Go to http://www.kfma.org.uk/FindaMarket.asp for more information.*

# The Directory

These great businesses have supported the making of this book; please support and enjoy them.

---

## Basil Wholefoods Limited

Head Office and Production Kitchen
28a St Johns Road
Tunbridge Wells
Kent
TN4 9NT
Telephone: 01892 802080
Website: www.foodbybasil.com

*An independent, family-run chain of cafés, passionate about creating imaginative salads, wholesome food, indulgent cakes and really great coffee.*

## The Beacon

Tea Garden Lane
Tunbridge Wells
TN3 9JH
Telephone: 01892 524252
Website: www.the-beacon.co.uk

*The Beacon is a restaurant with private dining rooms, bar and an outdoor terrace with stunning views across the acres of Kentish countryside it is at the heart of.*

## Bore Place

Bore Place Road
Chiddingstone
Kent
TN8 7AR
Telephone: 01732 463255
Website: www.boreplace.org

*Organic farm, market garden, venue and educational centre offering bespoke stays, events and an organic, locally sourced menu.*

## Caroline Kings

Website:
www.eataroundtonbridge.com

*Caroline Kings is a food blogger and champion of supporting local and independent. She is also a copywriter and member of the Guild of Food Writers.*

## Cocolicious

Stone Street
Cranbrook
Kent
TN17 3HF
Telephone: 01580 714954
Website: www.cocolicious.co.uk

*Cocolicious Pâtisserie Café is a little oasis nestled in the market town of Cranbrook offering truly delicious handmade sweet treats, savoury delights and artisan coffee.*

## Daily Bread

27-29 High Street
Rusthall
Kent
TN4 8RL
Telephone: 01892 457007
Website: dailybreadrusthall@gmail.com

*Family-friendly café focussing on homemade food with cakes and bread baked on site.*

## Framptons Café Bar & Kitchen

2 The Pantiles
Tunbridge Wells
TN2 5TJ
Telephone: 01892 530819
Website: www.framptonsbar.
co.uk/tunbridge_wells

*Independent café bar and kitchen, working with local suppliers, for the local community.*

## Fuggles Beer Café

Tonbridge
165 High Street
TN9 1BX
Telephone: 01732 666071
Website:
www.fugglesbeercafé.co.uk

*Created in 2013 with the aim of specialising in the best British & European beers we could find, coupled with great spirits, coffee, meats, cheeses and people in a relaxed and friendly environment.*

## Fuller's Farm Shop

1 The Barn
Bunny Lane
Eridge
Tunbridge Wells
Kent
TN3 9BY
Telephone: 01892 541238
Website: www.fullers-tw.co.uk

*Family butchers and farm shop, run with dedication to quality local produce and pride in the best customer service for over 45 years.*

## The Greyhound

Charcott
Leigh
Tonbridge
Kent TN11 8LG
Telephone: 01892 870275
Website:
www.thegreyhoundcharcott.co.uk

*Relaxed, traditional pub serving unbeatably local food and drink.*

## Gurkha Planet

16 Avebury Avenue
Tonbridge
TN9 1TN
Telephone: 01732 352074
Website: www.gurkhaplanet.co.uk

*Gurkha Planet serves food from around the world, with a particular emphasis on traditional Indian and Nepalese dishes, made by two acclaimed and highly experienced chefs.*

## Jane Beedle

Website: www.janebbakes.com
Email: jane@bakewithalegend.
com or jane@janebbakes.com

*Jane was a finalist in the 2016 series of the Great British Bake Off, and has been a keen supporter of Tree of Hope, particularly its 2018 Dine and Donate campaign.*

## The Lemon Grove

Email: hello@thelemongrove.net
Website: www.thelemongrove.net

*Inspired by Mediterranean flavours and textures, The Lemon Grove is run by Bruce McMichael, a food writer, communicator and cooking demonstrator who also sells a range of citrus-based sauces, spreads and chutneys.*

## Papermakers Arms

The Street
Plaxtol
Sevenoaks
TN15 0QJ
Telephone: 01732 810407
Website:
www.papermakersarms.com

*Friendly country pub and restaurant situated in the beautiful village of Plaxtol, offering great food using local and seasonal produce and an excellent choice of carefully selected beers, wines and gins.*

## The Plough at Ivy Hatch

High Cross Road
Ivy Hatch, Ightham
TN15 0NL
Telephone: 01732 810517
Website:
www.theploughivyhatch.co.uk

*Quintessential pub of Kent serving delicious plates, low intervention wine and craft ales. Friends to all including dogs!*

### The Poet at Matfield

Maidstone Road
Matfield
Kent
TN12 7JH
Telephone: 01892 722 416
Website:
www.thepoetatmatfield.co.uk

*Pub with restaurant in the heart of Kent, specialising in fine wines and gins alongside inventive cuisine and events including braai (South African barbecue) and gin festivals.*

### Rendez-Vous Restaurant

86 Camden Road
Tunbridge Wells
Kent
TN1 2QP
Telephone: 01892 525830
Website: www.rendezvoustw.co.uk

*A traditional brasserie-style restaurant with French influences in a friendly, relaxed environment.*

### Rustled Up

Email: Russell@rustledup.co.uk
Website: www.rustledup.co.uk

*Initially an Instagram account (@ rustledup) documenting Russell Goad's passion for food, who now holds supper clubs and private dining around Kent.*

### Sankey's Seafood Kitchen & Bar

39 Mt Ephraim
Tunbridge Wells
Kent TN4 8AA
Telephone: 01892 511422

### The Old Fishmarket by Sankey's

19 The Upper Pantiles
Tunbridge Wells
Kent TN2 5TN
Telephone: 01892 511422

### Sankey's Fishmongers Tonbridge

18 High Street
Tonbridge TN9 1EJ
Telephone: 01732 600118

### Sankey's Fishmongers Tunbridge Wells

9 Vale Road
Tunbridge Wells
Kent TN1 1BS
Telephone: 01892 511422
Website: www.sankeys.co.uk

*Sankey's is a family-owned business specialising in fresh fish and shellfish through retail, wholesale and restaurants.*

### Severien Vits

Blog:
www.morethanjustcarrots.com
Portfolio:
www.severienvits.myportfolio.com
Email: severien@
morethanjustcarrots.com

*Severien Vits is a food blogger and photographer, as well as mum to three kids and a keen advocate for nutritious homemade food and ways to eat healthily and happily for the whole family.*

### The Small Holding

Ranters Lane
Kilndown
Cranbrook
Kent
TN17 2SG
Telephone: 01892 809105
Email:
info@thesmallholding.restaurant

*Farm and kitchen showcasing the best of the beautiful Kent countryside and the home-grown ingredients that it produces.*

### Sulston's Kitchen

11 Quarry Hill Parade
Tonbridge
Kent
TN9 2HR
Telephone: 01732 366566
Website:
www.sulstonskitchen.co.uk

*Small family-run business in Tonbridge, established by Ben and Kirsty in 2014 as a YouTube channel. It has now developed into a small restaurant that specialises in delicious healthy food using seasonal produce and local suppliers.*

## The Swan at Chapel Down

Chapel Down Winery
Small Hythe Road
Tenterden
TN30 7NG
Telephone 01580 761616
Website:
www.swanchapeldown.co.uk

*The Swan is a restaurant with private dining and an open terrace across the award-winning Chapel Down vineyards. Group and private wine tastings and guided tours of the vineyard and winery are available.*

## The Twenty Six

15a Church Road
Southborough
Tunbridge Wells
TN4 0RX
Telephone: 01892 544607
Website: www.thetwenty-six.co.uk

*The Twenty Six is an intimate dining room with a private chef's table upstairs for a further 16 guests. Twenty Six chairs for twenty six people with a daily changing menu, inspired by the seasons.*

## Vittle and Swig

26-28 Camden Road
Tunbridge Wells
Kent
TN1 2PT
Telephone: 01892 544522
Website: www.vittleandswig.co.uk

*Modern British restaurant and bar with upstairs private rooms. Eclectic food, quirky interiors and a warm welcome.*

## The Warren Restaurant

5a High Street
Royal Tunbridge Wells
Kent
TN2 1UL
Telephone: 01892 328191
Website: thewarren.restaurant

*The Warren Restaurant is an extension of The Crowborough Estate, holding stock of Sussex cattle, Boer goats, fallow deer, wild boar and pigs among others which the restaurant draws on for its ever-changing seasonal menus. A genuine blend of traditional and contemporary British cooking.*

## Whiting and Hammond Pubs

## The Little Brown Jug

Chiddingstone Causeway
Tonbridge
Kent
TN11 8JJ
Telephone: 01892 870318
Website:
www.thelittlebrownjug.co.uk

## The Chaser Inn

Stumble Hill
Shipbourne
Tonbridge
Kent
TN11 9PE
Telephone: 01732 810360
Website: www.thechaser.co.uk

## The King's Head

2 Westerham Road
Bessels Green
Sevenoaks
Kent
TN13 2QA
Telephone: 01732 452081
Website:
www.kingsheadbesselsgreen.co.uk

*Award-winning company with eight family-run pubs across Kent and Sussex, started by Brian Whiting who joined forces with Chris Hammond to begin a venture focused on great food and drink.*

## Wholefood Wakeup

Website:
www.wholefoodwakeup.com
Instagram: @wholefoodwakeup

*Plant-based cooking workshops, delicious and creative dairy-free and gluten-free food, and vegan recipe consulting by health coach and food lover Debbie Stranack.*